12^{95}
¢

History and Structure

Studies in Contemporary German Social Thought
Thomas McCarthy, general editor

Alfred Schmidt, *History and Structure: An Essay on Hegelian-Marxist and Structuralist Theories of History,* 1981

Hans-Georg Gadamer, *Reason in the Age of Science,* 1982

Joachim Ritter, *Hegel and the French Revolution: Essays on the* Philosophy of Right, 1982

Theodor W. Adorno, *Prisms,* 1982

The MIT Press, Cambridge, Massachusetts, London, England

History and Structure

An Essay on Hegelian-Marxist and
Structuralist Theories of History

Alfred Schmidt
Translated by Jeffrey Herf

This book was set in Baskerville by Graphic Composition, Inc. and printed and
bound by The Murray Printing Co. in the United States of America.

Library of Congress Cataloging in Publication Data

Schmidt, Alfred, 1931–
    History and structure.

    (Studies in contemporary German social thought)
    Translation of: Geschichte und Struktur.
    Includes bibliographical references and index.
    1. Marx, Karl, 1818–1883. 2. Hegel, Georg
Wilhelm Friedrich, 1770–1831. 3. History—
Philosophy. 4. Dialectical materialism.
5. Althusser, Louis. 6. Structuralism. I. Title.
II. Series.
B3305.M74S3313   193   81–12324
ISBN 0–262–19198–9   AACR2

Contents

Series Foreword

From Hegel and Marx, Dilthey and Weber, to Freud and the Frankfurt School, German social theory enjoyed an undisputed preeminence. After the violent break brought about by National Socialism and World War II, this tradition has recently come to life again, and indeed to such an extent that contemporary German social thought has begun to approach the heights earlier attained. One important element in this renaissance has been the rapid and extensive translation into German of English-language works in the humanities and the social sciences, with the result that social thought in Germany is today markedly influenced by ideas and approaches of Anglo-American origin. Unfortunately, efforts in the other direction, the translation and reception of German works into English, have been sporadic at best. This series is intended to correct that imbalance.

The term *social thought* is here understood very broadly to include not only sociological and political thought as such but also the social-theoretical concerns of history and philosophy, psychology and linguistics, aesthetics and theology. The term *contemporary* is also to be construed broadly: though our attention will be focused primarily on postwar thinkers, we shall also publish works by and on earlier thinkers whose influence on contemporary German social thought is pervasive. The series will begin with translations of works by authors whose names are already widely recognized in English-speaking countries—

Series Foreword

Adorno, Bloch, Gadamer, Habermas, Marcuse, Ritter—and by authors of similar accomplishment who are not yet so familiar outside of Germany—Blumenberg, Peukert, Schmidt, Theunissen, Tugendhat. Subsequent volumes will also include monographs and collections of essays written in English on German social thought and its concerns.

To understand and appropriate other traditions is to broaden the horizons of one's own. It is our hope that this series, by tapping a neglected store of intellectual riches and making it accessible to the English-speaking public, will expand the frame of reference of our social and political discourse.

Thomas McCarthy

Acknowledgments

I should like to thank Thomas McCarthy for reading the first draft of this translation and offering numerous suggestions and for his encouragement and support from the beginning of this project; Andy Buchwalter and Fred van Gelder for their assistance and suggestions; Alfred Schmidt for his encouragement; and Christoph Schlotterer of Hanser Verlag in Munich for his editorial support.

Translator's Introduction

It is remarkable that the extensive controversy over structuralist Marxism in the English-speaking world has provoked no book-length critique by a critical theorist that confronts structuralist claims on a philosophical plane. Alfred Schmidt's *History and Structure* fills this gap. In West Germany today Schmidt is the leading exponent of and commentator on the critical theory of the Frankfurt School as formulated by Max Horkheimer, Theodor Adorno, and Herbert Marcuse. Only one of his books, *The Concept of Nature in Marx*, has been translated into English, however, and thus the full scope of his work remains largely unknown to the Anglo-American audience.[1] His other books and essays over the last two decades include critical studies of Feuerbach, Schopenhauer, Nietzsche, Horkheimer, and Marcuse as well as discussions of the philosophy of history, the history of nineteenth- and twentieth-century philosophical materialism, and Marx, in particular the epistemological aspects of his critique of political economy.[2] Like the first generation of critical theorists, Schmidt's understanding of Marx and Marxism freely incorporates non-Marxist traditions with the aim of preserving the critical intentions that are lost when Marxism ceases to be a critical theory of society and becomes instead a "science of legitimation."[3] Hence it is hardly surprising that he took up the challenge posed by Althusser's militant reaffirmation of Marxism's scientific pretensions.

Schmidt's response to Althusser's Marxism is the most sustained to have emerged from any theorist associated with the Frankfurt School. It comprises several essays written in the late 1960s, including *History and Structure*, and a later work, *Die Kritische Theorie als Geschichtsphilosophie* (Critical Theory as a Philosophy of History 1976).[4] *History and Structure* is more than a valuable intervention in the controversy over Althusser's Marxism. It also offers an interpretation of the mature Marx and the influence of Hegel on Marx's critique of political economy and in doing so recasts some of the terms of the debate between what Alvin Gouldner called "the two Marxisms."[5] This translation should both encourage further interest in Schmidt's other works and alert an English-speaking audience to the existence of the extensive philosophically informed discussion of Marx which has taken place in West Germany in the last decade and which remains largely untranslated.[6]

In *History and Structure* Schmidt emphasizes the enduring influence of Hegel on Marx's mature critique of political economy and thus reaffirms one of the major themes of "Hegelian-Marxism." However, the way in which he locates this influence distinguishes his analysis from that of, for example, Lukács's *History and Class Consciousness* or Marcuse's *Reason and Revolution*. Whereas Hegelian-Marxists have traditionally stressed Hegel's *Phenomenology of the Mind*, and thus the enduring significance of the themes of alienation, objectification, and reification of consciousness and social existence in Marx's *Grundrisse* and *Capital*, Schmidt, without rejecting this view, gives added weight to the importance of Hegel's *The Science of Logic*.[7] To the reader who has been accustomed to assigning the systematic aspects of Hegel's work to the pre-history of Soviet Marxism's science of society and nature, this is a startling tack for a Hegelian-Marxist to take.[8] Just when it appeared that the two Marxisms could be neatly correlated with two Marxs, Schmidt and others have come along to wreak havoc with this schema. Before turning to

Schmidt's own contribution, a brief discussion of the two Marx-isms is in order.

Gouldner succinctly summarized the dispute between Marx-ism as critique (or critical Marxism) and Marxism as science (or scientific Marxism): The former affirms the positive impact of Hegel, in particular, and German Idealism, in general, on the young and old Marx, stressing the importance of the young Marx and the problem of alienation in Marx's mature political economy. The latter sees Hegelian and idealist influences as un-fortunate "ideological" baggage supposedly jettisoned by Marx after a radical break (*coupure épistémologique*) with Hegel. This break pointed to scientific "structuralist" methodology which came to fruition in the post-humanist, post-historicist mature political economy of *Capital*.[9] These textual disputes have never been purely academic affairs. Since the codification of Soviet Marxism in the 1920s and the accompanying self-understand-ing of Marxism-Leninism as a science of the laws of society and nature, "Western Marxism" has repeatedly expressed itself in fleeting explosions of individual and collective subjectivity and activity—the worker's councils in Central Europe following World War I, the Hungarian revolution of 1956, and the New Left in Europe and North America in the 1960s.[10] The intensity with which the dispute over the interpretation of Marx has been conducted cannot be understood without taking this historical experience into account, an experience including both the his-tory of Stalinism and the revolt against it.[11] However, although the notion of "the two Marxisms" sheds a great deal of light on the matter, it should not be taken to overly schematic conclu-sions. As Maurice Merleau-Ponty pointed out in *The Adventures of the Dialectic*, the objectivistic scientism of Soviet Marxism also allowed plenty of room for subjectivity of the Party, an "authori-tarian voluntarism" in Marcuse's words.[12] On the other hand, as Schmidt has argued in his *Drei Studien uber Materialismus* (1977) (*Three Studies on Materialism*), philosophical materialism in both

Marxist and non-Marxist incarnations recalls individual happiness, individual needs and satisfactions, individual willing in contrast to the mythology of a justificatory idealist metaphysic of History.[13]

The situation is further complicated by the fact that some important exponents or sympathetic interpreters of the critical tradition agree with some of the contentions put forward by structuralists. For example, while fundamentally disagreeing with Althusser's intentions, Jürgen Habermas, Albrecht Wellmer, Jean Baudrillard, Cornelius Castoriadis, and E. P. Thompson have in varying fashions argued that Marx's mature political economy presents a "latent positivism," "a mirror of production," a rationalistic bias or a "prison of political economy"—all of which provided the soil in which the authoritarian Marxism of the Stalinist tradition could take root.[14] Along similar lines, Paul Breines and Andrew Arato have suggested that the history of Marxism can be understood as a cyclical alternation between romantic and enlightenment-rationalistic poles, a cycle first made manifest in the biography of Marx himself.[15] What these authors within the Hegelian-Marxist tradition have in common is an implicit, at times explicit, exasperation with Marx's critique of political economy because it succumbs to more than it criticizes the life and culture of capitalism. It attempts to do the impossible, namely to force the multiple dimensions of politics, law, experience, feeling, culture, race, sex, language, or social interaction into the one dimension defined by the categories of political economy. No longer interested in fighting a battle of the texts in order to rescue Marx's critique of political economy from structuralist misinterpretations, some members of the Hegelian-Marxist tradition are pointing toward a post-Marxist critical social theory. With a few notable exceptions,[16] critical Marxists in Great Britain and the United States have in fact largely given up the ghost of Marx's political economy. The dialectical unity of philosophy, history, and political economy that

Marx sought has, at least within the English-language discussion of Marx and Marxism, most emphatically split asunder. To critical Marxist (and Habermasian) ears, the sound of Marx's political economy rings of orthodoxy and scientism.

For example, Thompson sees in Marx's mature political economy an "unreconstructed Hegelianism" through which a ghostly autonomy is bestowed on "capital in the totality of its relations," a capital which "posits this and that, creates this and that." He agrees with Schmidt that the influence of Hegel persisted in the mature Marx, yet, unlike Schmidt, he sees this influence as disastrous, as the harbinger of the closed ahistorical system that "dialectical materialism" was to become. Thompson regards as a disservice Althusser's efforts to "thrust historical materialism back into the prison of the categories of Political Economy."[17] In his view, experience, values, culture, feeling were stifled in the Stalinist discourse of political economy and Hegelian rigor and system.

Schmidt is no less aware of the experience of Stalinism than Thompson. Whereas Thompson appeals to the British tradition of social history against the imperialistic claims of Marxist scientism, Schmidt appeals to the German tradition of dialectical social theory—which includes Hegel and political economy—as his counter to the Althusserian project.

In this context, Alfred Schmidt's defense of the mature Marx, his refusal to view the young Marx as the exponent of an ahistorical ontology, and his insistence on the indispensability of the critique of political economy to a contemporary critical theory of society will strike some as out of step and unfashionable, which in a sense they are. But they certainly do not constitute a renewal of orthodoxy and scientism. Nor do they pose yet another in a depressing series of false alternatives: Marxism or romanticism, Hegel or political economy, alienation or surplus value, history or structure. In Schmidt's view, the "and" in the title of this essay belongs between the preceding conceptual pairs as well. Schmidt's refusal to accept the validity of Althusser's interpretation of Marx recalls the Adorno sentence which he cites: "The shrinking of the consciousness of historical continuity is more than an aspect of decline—it is necessarily linked with the principle of progress in bourgeois society."[18] Marxism as a tradition is not immune from the spirit of progress. It can forget the critical-historical dimension of Marx's mature work just as easily as it can forget Hegel. Schmidt's intent in *History and Structure* is not to add to the mountain of Marxology but to affirm the historical consciousness which structuralism denies.

I would like now to sketch a few of the basic themes which have consistently appeared in Schmidt's work.[19] The concept of "*second nature,*" a crucial concept for the first generation of the Frankfurt School, is, in Schmidt's view "the most important methodological idea of the materialist dialectic." It seeks to distinguish "first nature," that is, the interaction between human beings and nature which is at the basis of all human existence, from "second nature," or the form this interaction assumes in a historically specific society.[20] Against Engels's effort to develop a supra-historical dialectic applicable equally to nature and society, Schmidt stresses the sociohistorical character of Marx's concept of nature.[21] Moreover, following Horkheimer and Adorno, he places the *subject-object dialectic* at the center of his social theory. The subject transforms nature and him/herself through labor and in the very process falls under the sway of second nature, a blind necessity set against its creators. Marx's materialism, Schmidt argues, far from acquiescing to the appearance of iron historical laws, constituted "a unified critical judgment on previous history, to the effect that men have allowed themselves to be degraded into objects of the blind and mechanical process of its economic dynamic.[22] Previous history thus remains *pre-history*, one not yet guided by the practice of consciously acting subjects. Thus Marx's concept of labor and praxis preserves the *problem of constitution* of the world by the knowing

subject as presented in Kant and Hegel and upholds "the idealist moment of creation and the moment of the independence of
consciousness from external being."[23] For Marx and Hegel,
Schmidt claims, the "highest form of epistemology" is contained
in the theory of pre-history as the critique of second nature.

This whole problem of constitution was repressed by "orthodox" Marxism which thus ceased to be a critical theory of society. It elevated the "laws" of second nature, the existence of
which depended, in Marx's view, on the continued existence of
specific social conditions and human unconsciousness, into laws
of history in general. "What in Marx is the object of critique, is
in Stalinism raised to the rank of a scientific norm."[24] While this
procedure had its uses in the creation of state religions, it had
nothing to do with an "originally critical and radical historical
theory."[25] The latter seeks to uncover the human activity now
submerged in the established facts. Schmidt agrees with Adorno's
assertion that "the strongest motives of Marxist theory" do not
suggest the ontologization of "natural laws" in history but rather
their abolition.[26]

In the context of the Hegelian-Marxist tradition, Schmidt's
treatment of Marx is unusual in its emphasis on the critique of
political economy and on what Schmidt refers to as Marx's "second appropriation of Hegel."[27] This refers to Marx's incorporation of Hegel's *Philosophy of Nature, Lectures on the Philosophy of
History*, and, above all, *The Science of Logic*, as distinguished from
the *Phenomenology of the Mind*, a work whose impact was decisive
for the Paris manuscripts of 1844. The importance of Hegel's
Logic for Marx's *Capital* was emphasized by Lenin in his *Philosophical Notebooks*, but this argument has remained undeveloped,
certainly within the critical tradition. Schmidt and other critical
West German commentators on Marx of the past fifteen years,
such as Hans-Jurgen Krahl, Helmut Reichelt, and Michael
Theunissen, have offered the most extensive development of
this interpretation since Lenin and have done so in an episte-

mological framework decidedly other than that set by Lenin.[28] Schmidt argues that what has too often been criticized as the objectivism or scientism of the late Marx is rather the product of Marx's effort to grasp the specific, historical character of the abstractions through which capitalist social relations find expression. Where Hegel saw the movement of categories as the manifestation of a supra-historical *Geist*, Marx saw the categories of bourgeois political economy as "finite, transient" products of the finite and transient reality of capitalism.[29]

Why then is Marx's critique of political economy so often characterized as the most objectivistic and most ahistorical aspect of his thought? The reason, Schmidt argues, is that with the exception of some of Horkheimer's essays in the 1930s, the important distinction between "inquiry" (*Forschung*) and "presentation" (*Darstellung*) has largely been ignored by commentators on Marx's *Capital*.[30] "The correct understanding of Marx's method in *Capital*," Schmidt wrote in 1967, "stands and falls with the concept of presentation."[31] The "mode of presentation" (*Darstellungsweise*) in *Capital* does not follow the narrative history of its development but begins with the finished forms—money, commodities, exchange value, etc.—in which the system reproduces itself. Hence in the first volume of *Capital*, it is not until chapter 24 that the historical presuppositions of the analysis of commodity fetishism developed in chapter 1 are presented. The logical construction of Marx's categorical analysis of capitalism is in reverse order to the actual, historical sequence in which the social relations underlying these categories developed. Schmidt emphasizes, however, that while the "mode of presentation" does not parallel the actual course of events, it does presuppose them and is not intended to replace them or to establish a methodological primacy of structure over history. The categories of Marx's critique of political economy in *Capital* and the *Grundrisse* ought not be separated from the historic reality of capitalism. The nonidentity of essence and appearance that Marx took over from Hegel's *Logic* applies to capitalist commodity production rather than to social life in general. It is with the development of capitalism that the products of human labor become commodities, that relations between human beings assume the appearance of relations between things, and that the personal forms of domination that characterized precapitalist society assume abstract and impersonal forms. Marx's critique of political economy aims at recovering the constitutive human praxis and subjectivity that lay beneath the surface appearances of capitalism. It is a continuation of his fundamental project: the critique of "second nature." Hence, although Marx did not write a philosophical epistemology, his critique of political economy, Schmidt argues, contains a "richness in philosophically important insights and problems" that remains to be examined.[32] As a theory of social consciousness and unconsciousness, Marx's work is simultaneously social theory and epistemology.

Schmidt's understanding of Marx's critique of political economy as part of a critical theory of society as well as his critique of structuralism draw heavily on Horkheimer's distinction between traditional and critical theory. Briefly, Horkheimer argued that unlike traditional theory, which assumed that social relations did not at all enter into its own methods and intentions, critical theory is defined by the unflinching reflection on its own historical and social determination.[33] Critical theory views society from the standpoint of what it judges to be the interests of individuals in a free and rational organization of social life. These interests are not external to the process of cognition. Rather they constitute it and see to it that theory examines existing facts from the perspective of their possible transformation. In short, a critical theory views existing facts as themselves historical products. That they appear to be natural phenomena, that history up to the present appears to be a process without a subject, that social being determines social consciousness, or that individuals appear as personifications of economic categories, all of these circumstances are aspects of "pre-history," an era which presupposes the very absence of the historical consciousness which critical theory seeks to nurture. Only when individuals collectively control the life processes that have previously ruled them with the force of blind fate will human freedom for the individual be possible. Then historical materialism will cease to be the proper explanation of historical and social processes. As Horkheimer put it, "The critical recognition of the categories dominating social life contains simultaneously their condemnation,"[34] for critical theory incorporates Kant's idea of human autonomy:

A consciously critical attitude . . . is part of the development of society: construing the course of history as the necessary product of an economic mechanism simultaneously contains both a protest against this order of things, a protest generated by the order itself, and the idea of self-determination for the human race, that is the idea of a state of affairs in which man's actions no longer flow from a mechanism but from his own decision. The judgment passed on the necessity inherent in the previous course of events implies here a struggle to change it from a blind to a meaningful necessity.[35]

The passage to a free and rational society is not at all guaranteed by blind necessity. Rather it depends on the moral decision of individuals. To elevate history without a subject to a scientific norm, as traditional and structuralist theories do to make "the claim that events are absolutely necessary, means in the last analysis the same thing as the claim to be really free here and now: resignation in practice."[36] Thus Schmidt takes up Horkheimer's argument that the good society, a socialist society, is historically possible but is not guaranteed by a logic immanent in history; it can be created only by individuals who have consciously chosen this option.[37] As Horkheimer argued, however, the "free subject consciously forming social existence" has not existed in pre-history. To bring this subject into existence is both

the means and end of bringing about a rationally organized socialist society.[38] Schmidt notes that there is an ironic agreement
here with the structuralist "scientistic objectivism," which claims
that a subject in history is not recognizable. But as Schmidt puts
it, the issue is "not only one of knowledge but also of existence,"[39]
and here critical theory and structuralism part ways.

The fundamental points of Schmidt's critique of structuralism
are implicit in Horkheimer's critique of traditional theory. In his
1969 essay, "The Structuralist Attack on History," Schmidt developed these points, foreshadowing the basic themes of the
present work. Structuralism ceases to be a critical theory of society precisely because it represses the historical dimension of
theory. For example, where Marx saw ideology in capitalist society as laying in appearances that could be historically transcended, Althusser "naturalizes" the concept of ideology by
suggesting that it is a functional mystification of any social order.[40] Rather than confronting the dilemma of truth and ideology, Althusser replaces it with "the simple fiat of science." The
possibility of overcoming ideology is thereby ruled out from the
outset. Structuralism and structuralist Marxism thus become
unintentional apologies for a still unmastered "second nature."
Despite its bluster, its muscular attacks on "historicism" and "humanism," structuralism is marked above all by resignation to the
appearances of a historically specific absence of human activity.
It adds its voice to the conservative claim that the present has no
historical dimension. By conceptually ratifying the autonomy of
economic mechanisms over individual activity, structuralism has
thereby captured the spirit of the age—uncritically. While presenting itself as an illusionless science in contrast to a fuzzy humanism and historicism, structuralism is in actuality the illusion
of the epoch. As Adorno put it, in late capitalism, ideology is the
process of production itself.[41]

Thus Schmidt's critique is aimed at what has been described
as the "methodological dehistoricization of Marx's analysis of

capital"[42] fostered by the Althusser circle. In summary, it is not only Althusser's attack on the notion of a unified subject in the historical process which leads him to grasp history as a sequence of supra-historical structures and seek laws applicable to history in a universal schematic sense. His misunderstanding of Marx's method in *Capital* also contributes to his effort to establish Marxism as a general theory of history. Only the structuralist interpretation of Marx's political economy allows Althusser to graft fundamental structuralist assumptions onto a Marxist theory of history. It is only by forgetting that Marx's analysis of capitalism points to the historical origins of supra-historical appearances that Althusser is able to shift Marx's theory to the level of an analysis of laws of society in general.

If, as Schmidt and other West German interpreters of Marx have argued, Marx's critique of political economy is a systematic presentation of the deformation of social relationships by capitalism, then its applicability is limited to capitalist societies. It is just this methodological restriction, these authors argue, that structuralist Marxism does not consider, and hence it wrongly transforms Marx's theory of capitalism into a general theory of society. Marx's abstraction from those aspects of individuals as subjects that are unrelated to their activity in the process of capital accumulation and realization was, they argue, never intended as a general theorem of social life but as a critical statement about what human beings are reduced to in this particular society. Althusser's view of Marxism as a general theory of history thus undermines Marx's *critique* of political economy. The greater importance of Hegel's *Logic* as distinct from his *Phenomenology* in Marx's mature political economy does not, they argue, signal a repression of his anthropological and epistemological insights into the human subjectivity as expressed in labor. Rather Marx took Hegel's *Logic* as a model which prefigured his own view of the value realizing itself in the developed capitalist system. The element that safeguards this procedure from becoming what Thompson denounces as "idealist metaphysics" is, according to these authors, the historical nature of Marx's method, that is, the consciousness that it is dealing with the particular reality of capitalism. Althusserian structuralism begins, they argue, with the dehistoricization of Marx's critique of political economy, its transformation into that against which it was directed: a general (Marxist) theory of history.[43]

To this reconsideration of the late Hegel and Marx, Schmidt brings his interest in thinkers, such as Feuerbach, Schopenhauer, Nietzsche, Horkheimer, and Adorno, who have defended the individual and the particular against the systems in theory and society that would absorb the subject completely. It is rare to find a thinker like Schmidt who tries to capture the letter and spirit of both Marx's political economy and Nietzsche's views on the uses and abuses of history.[44] Russell Jacoby has recently written that "asceticism is the conceptual center of gravity of orthodox Marxism."[45] This "puritanism of knowledge"[46] is evident, he continues, in the fear of the unstructured, the taboo on utopia and romanticism and the "cold passion of science and authority" that marks structural Marxism.[47] In the Marxist tradition, advocacy of what Ernst Bloch called the "cold current" of technocratic Marxism has usually been associated with Marx's *Capital*. The paradoxical point of the present work is that Schmidt comes to the defense of what Bloch called the "warm current"[48] of Marxism in part through reinterpretation of this supposedly "cold" text. He defends the individual subject without neglecting the power of structures in pre-history. The reader should find his discussion helpful in overcoming some of the facile dichotomies between history and structure, subject and object, that have surfaced in the English language discussion of Marx and structuralism. To the degree that Schmidt has been successful in channeling the "warm" historical current into the seemingly cold and ahistorical waters of Marx's later work, he has made an important contribution to contemporary discussions of Marx, Marxist historiography, and critical theory.

Notes

1. Alfred Schmidt, *The Concept of Nature in Marx*, trans. Ben Fowkes (London: New Left Books, 1971).

2. See, for example, *Emanzipatorische Sinnlichkeit: Ludwig Feuerbachs Anthropologischer Materialismus* (Munich: Hanser Verlag, 1973); *Zur Idee der Kritischen Theorie* (Munich: Hanser Verlag, 1974); *Die Kritische Theorie als Geschichtsphilosophie* (Munich: Hanser Verlag, 1976); *Drei Studien über Materialismus* (Munich: Hanser Verlag, 1977); and Walter Post, *Was Ist Materialismus* (Munich: Hanser Verlag, 1975); editor, *Beiträge zur marxistischen Erkenntnistheorie* (Frankfurt/Main: Suhrkamp Verlag, 1969).

3. On this development see Oskar Negt's essay "Marxismus als Legitimationswissenschaft. Zur Genese der stalinistischen Philosophie," in *Nikolai Bucharin/Abram Deborin: Kontroversen über dialektischen und mechanistischen Materialismus* (Frankfurt/Main: Suhrkamp, 1969), pp. 7–48.

4. Schmidt, *Die Kritische Theorie.*

5. Alvin Gouldner, *The Two Marxisms* (New York, 1980). See also Alvin Gouldner "The Two Marxisms," in *For Sociology* (Harmondsworth, Middlesex, England: Penguin, 1973), pp. 425–462.

6. An introduction to some of the academic Marxist discussions in West Germany is offered in Urs Jaeggi and Axel Honneth, eds., *Theorien des Historischen Materialismus* (Frankfurt/Main: Suhrkamp Verlag, 1977), and *Arbeit, Handlung, Normativität: Theorien des Historischen II*, (Frankfurt/Main: Suhrkamp Verlag, 1980).

7. Works in the Hegelian-Marxist tradition stressing the importance of Hegel's *Phenomenology* in the mature Marx include the following: George Lukács, *The Young Hegel*, trans. Rodney Livingstone (Cambridge, Mass: MIT Press, 1976); Jean Hyppolite, *Studies on Marx and Hegel*, ed. and trans. John O'Neill (New York: Harper Torchbooks, 1969); and Herbert Marcuse, *Reason and Revolution* (Boston: Beacon Press, 1960).

8. On the Soviet Marxist incorporation of Hegel the systematic thinker see Iring Fetscher, *Marx and Marxism*, trans. John Hargreaves (New York: Herder and Herder, 1971). Helmut Fleischer, in his *Marxism and History*, trans. Eric Mosbacher (New York: Harper Torchbooks, 1973), wrote, "The Marxist view of history is pragmatical, and involves a radical break with the idea of history as a whole. In his historical thinking Marx did not remain a Hegelian. He says nothing whatever to justify the view that he 'deified' history" (p. 71). Schmidt, on the

Translator's Introduction

other hand, maintains that Marx did remain a Hegelian and did not deify the historical process.

9. Gouldner, "The Two Marxisms," pp. 430–433.

10. For the original statement of the relationship between Hegelian-Marxism and revolutionary practice see Karl Korsch, *Marxism and Philosophy*, trans. Fred Halliday (London: New Left Books, 1970). See also the discussion of "the cycle in the history of Marxism" in Andrew Arato and Paul Breines, *The Young Lukács and the Origins of the Western Marxism* (New York: Seabury Press, 1979), pp. 210–226.

11. As Paul Piccone has written ("Reading the Grundrisse: Beyond 'Othodox' Marxism," *Theory and Society* 2 (Summer 1975):236),

The truth or falsity of the contraposition a few years ago of the young Marx of the 1844 Manuscripts to the mature and "scientific" Marx of *Capital* is not to be found solely in well-known or obscure texts, but in the socio-historical context of Stalinist terror and in the political task of introducing a humanist dimension within an otherwise hopeless context—and it is only to be expected that the main thrust of "humanistic" Marxism since World War II has come primarily from Eastern Europe. Similarly, the truth or falsity of "dialectical materialism" or of the Althusserian reinterpretation is not be be ascertained merely by pointing out how often Marx uses Hegelian notions in his mature writings, but also in terms of the legitimating function that official Marxist ideology, or even Althusserianism, performs for the Soviet Union or for the French Communist Party.

Understanding the political uses of different interpretations of Marx, however, should complement and not replace a careful examination of the original sources. On the "work of selective tradition" see Raymond Williams's suggestive comments in his *Marxism and Literature* (New York: Oxford University Press, 1977). The German term *Rezeptionsgeschichte*, or "history of reception," suggests both the historical and hermeneutic dimensions that the present work aims at.

12. Maurice Merleau-Ponty, *The Adventures of the Dialectic*, trans. Joseph Bien (Evanston: Northwestern University Press, 1973); see also James Miller's fine study, *History and Human Existence: From Marx to Merleau-Ponty* (Berkeley, Los Angeles and London: University of California Press, 1979).

13. Schmidt, *Drei Studien über Materialismus*, especially "Zum begriff des Glücks in der materialistischen Philosophie," pp. 135–195.

14. See Jürgen Habermas, *Theory and Practice*, trans. John Viertel (Boston: Beacon Press, 1973) and *Knowledge and Human Interests* trans. Jeremy Shapiro (Boston: Beacon Press, 1971); Abrecht Wellmer, *Critical Theory of Society*, trans. John Cumming (New York: Herder and Herder, 1971); Jean Baudrillard, *The Mirror of Production*, trans. Mark Poster (St. Louis: Telos Press, 1975); Cornelius Castoriadis, "On the History of the Workers' Movement," *Telos* 30 (Winter 1976–1977): 3–42 and *L'Institution imaginaire de la societe* (Paris, 1975); and E. P.

Thompson, "The Poverty of Theory or an Orrery of Errors," in *The Poverty of Theory and Other Essays* (New York and London: Monthly Review Press, 1978), pp. 1–210.

15. Arato and Breines, *The Young Lukács*.

16. See Paul Mattick, *Marx and Keynes: The Limits of the Mixed Economy* (Boston: Porter Sargent, 1969); Giacomo Marramao, "Political Economy and Critical Theory," *Telos* 24 (Summer 1975): 56–80; Russell Jacoby, "The Politics of the Crisis Theory: Towards a Critique of Automatic Marxism II," *Telos* 23 (Spring 1975): 3–52. Also see Jacoby's excellent critique of structuralist and other varieties of Marxist scientism: "What Is Conformist Marxism," *Telos* 45 (Fall 1980): 19–43. See also Perry Anderson, *Arguments Within English Marxism* (London: Verso Editions, 1980) for a critical response to Thompson.

17. Thompson, "The Poverty of Theory," p. 68. Thompson's essay is, in my opinion, one of the great literary and political statements of the postwar European Left. It should be read together with Schmidt's essay. Like Schmidt, Thompson sees structuralism as the illusion of the epoch. In his view, the historical background for structuralism in thought was the Cold War.

18. Theodor Adorno, "Was bedeutet Aufarbeitung der Vergangenheit," in *Erziehung zur Mündigkeit* (Frankfurt/Main: Suhrkamp Verlag, 1970), p. 13.

19. Many of these ideas are presented in *The Concept of Nature in Marx*.

20. Alfred Schmidt, "Zum Erkenntnisbegriff der Kritik der politischen Ökonomie," in *Kritik der politischen Okonomie heute: 100 Jahre Kapitel*, eds. Walter Euchner and Alfred Schmidt (Frankfurt/Main: Europaische Verlagsanstalt, 1968), p. 29.

21. For Schmidt's discussion of the denial of the socio-historical character of Marx's concept of nature in "dialectical materialism" see "Appendix: On the Relation Between History and Nature in Dialectical Materialism," in *The Concept of Nature in Marx*, pp. 165–196.

22. Schmidt, *Marx's Concept of Nature*, p. 41.

23. Ibid., p. 114.

24. Ibid., p. 192.

25. Ibid.

26. Theodor Adorno, *Negative Dialectic*, trans. E. B. Ashton (New York: Seabury Press, 1973), p. 355.

27. Schmidt, "Zum Erkenntnisbegriff der Kritik der politischen Okonomie," p. 32.

Translator's Introduction

28. See Hans Jurgen Krahl, "Zur Wesenslogik der Marxschen Warenanalyse," in *Konstitution und Klassenkampf* (Frankfurt/Main: Verlag Neue Kritik, 1971) pp. 31–81; Helmut Reichelt, *Zur logischen Struktur des Kapitalbegriffs bei Karl Marx* (Frankfurt/Main, 1970); Michael Theunissen, "Krise der Macht. Thesen zur Theorie des dialektischen Widerspruchs," in *Hegel-Jahrbuch 1974*, ed. W. R. Beyer (Cologne, 1975); and Rüdiger Bubner, "Logik und Kapital. Zur Methode einer 'Kritik der politische Okonomie," in *Dialektik und Wissenschaft* (Frankfurt/Main, 1973). For a good summation of these interpretations see Axel Honneth, "Geschichte und Interaktionsverhältnisse: Zur strukturalistischen Deutung des Historischen Materialismus," in Jaeggi and Honneth, *Theorien des Historischen Materialismus*, pp. 405–449. Krahl, a leading theorist and participant in the German New Left, died in an automobile crash in 1970. His essay "Zur Wesenslogik . . . " was originally delivered in Adorno's seminar in 1966–67 and exerted a marked influence on subsequent efforts. Like Schmidt's *History and Structure*, Krahl's essay combines a discussion of the impact of Hegel's *Logic* in Marx's *Capital* along with an extensive discussion of the heritage of German Idealism and Romanticism—Kant, Hegel, Nietzsche, Novalis—a juxtaposition which, as far as I know, is unique to the West German discussion of Marx.

29. Schmidt, "Zum Erkenntnisbegriff der Kritik . . . , p. 34.

30. Schmidt has commented extensively on Horkheimer. See the following: *Zur Idee der Kritischen Theorie . . .* ; *Die Kritische Theorie als Geschichtsphilosophie*; and "Die geistige Physiognomie Max Horkheimers," in *Drei Studien über Materialismus*, pp. 81–134.

31. Schmidt, "Zum Erkenntnis der Kritik . . . , p. 35.

32. Ibid., p. 42.

33. See Max Horkheimer, "Traditional and Critical Theory," in *Critical Theory*, trans. Mathew J. O'Connell et al. (New York: Herder and Herder, 1972), pp. 188–252; and Schmidt's discussion in *Zur Idee einer Kritischen Theorie*, pp. 32–35, and in *Die Kritische Theorie als Geschichtsphilosophie*, pp. 81–99.

34. Horkheimer, "Traditional and Critical Theory," p. 208.

35. Ibid., p. 229.

36. Ibid., p. 231.

37. See Max Horkheimer, *Notizen 1950 bis 1969 und Dammerung. Notizen in Deutschland* (Frankfurt/Main: Athenaum Fischer Taschenbuch Verlag, 1974), p. 253. Cited by Schmidt in *Die Kritische Theorie als Geschictsphilosophie*, p. 99.

38. Ibid., p. 269–270.

39. Schmidt, *Die Kritische Theorie als Geschichtsphilosophie*, p. 99.

Translator's Introduction

40. Alfred Schmidt, "Der strukturalistische Angriff auf die Geschichte," in Schmidt, *Beiträge zur marxistischen Erkenntnistheorie*, pp. 194–265. Aside from *History and Structure*, this essay is Schmidt's most extensive discussion of structuralism, in particular of Levi-Strauss.

41. Theodor Adorno, *Prisms*, trans. Samuel and Shierry Weber (London: Neville Spearman, 1967), pp. 30–31.

42. Honneth, "Geschichte und Interaktionsverhältnisse . . . ," p. 442.

43. Ibid., pp. 436–442. See also J. P. Arnason, *Zwischen Natur und Gesellschaft. Studien zu einer kritischen Theorie des Subjekts* (Frankfurt/Main, Cologne, 1976).

44. But it is becoming less rare to find authors working on the problem of Marx and Nietzsche. Some recent contributions are: David Bathrick and Paul Breines, "Marx und/oder Nietzsche. Anmerkungen zur Krise des Marxismus," in Reinhold Grimm and Jost Hermand, eds. *Karl Marx und Friedrich Nietzsche* (Frankfurt/Main: Athenaum Verlag, 1978), pp. 119–135; James Miller, *History and Human Existence*, pp. 140–155; and Gillian Rose, *The* Melancholy Science: *An Introduction to the Thought of Theodor Adorno* (New York: Columbia University Press, 1978), especially pp. 18–26.

45. Russell Jacoby, "What is Conformist Marxism," *Telos* 45 (Fall 1980): 43.

46. Theodor Adorno et. al., *The Positivism Dispute in German Sociology* (London, 1976), pp. 55–56.

47. Jacoby, "What is Conformist Marxism," p. 43.

48. Ernst Bloch, *Geist der Utopie* (Frankfurt/Main: Suhrkamp Verlag, 1964). For Schmidt's discussions of Bloch see *The Concept of Nature in Marx, Emanzipatorische Sinnlichkeit*, pp. 45–46; and *Drei Studien über Materialismus*, pp. 38–41.

History and Structure

The Possibility of Progress

When a scholar of the ancient culture forswears the company of men who believe in progress, he does quite right. For the greatness and goodness of ancient culture lie behind it, and historical education compels one to admit that they can never be fresh again; an unbearable stupidity or an equally insufferable fanaticism would be necessary to deny this. But men can *consciously* resolve to develop themselves toward a new culture; whilst formerly they only developed unconsciously and by chance, they can now create better conditions for the rise of human beings, for their nourishment, education, and instruction; they can administer the earth economically as a whole, and can generally weigh and restrain the powers of man. This new, conscious culture kills the old, which, regarded as a whole, has led an unconscious animal and plant life; it also kills distrust in progress—progress is *possible*. I must say that it is over-hasty and almost nonsensical to believe that progress must *necessarily* follow; but how could one deny that it is possible? On the other hand, progress in the sense and on the path of the old culture is not even thinkable. Even if romantic fantasy has also constantly used the word "progress" to denote its aims (for instance, circumscribed primitive national cultures), it borrows the picture of it in any case from the past; its thoughts and ideas on this subject are entirely without originality.

Nietzsche, *Human, All-Too-Human*, Aphorism 24.

The Theme: History without Structure or Structure without History?

A growing exhaustion with history, especially in the West, characterizes the second half of the twentieth century. The highly polished research techniques of contemporary social science are increasingly dislodging historical thinking from the role it played in connection with the Enlightenment and German Idealism, in Dilthey and the traditional *Geisteswissenschaften*, in *Lebensphilosophie*, and even in existentialism. Herbert Luthy has offered a drastic yet apt characterization of the contemporary "mathematization of the social sciences" (which he includes among the "human sciences"):

The big computer, the status symbol of modern scholarship, is about to encompass the whole of the human sciences. Since Lévi-Strauss formulated the kinship structure of the Borero in terms of a model employing mathematical functions, a cultural sociology has emerged which represents a civilization as a closed communicative system, completely independent from the consciousness of individuals. It does so because it views individual consciousness as determined by this communications system. . . . At bottom, the disintegration of the human sciences stems from the illusion, pursued with a methodical obsessiveness, that it is possible to escape from the reality of the interpenetration of consciousness within human history and from the decisions concerning values and power which characterize this history, into the ahistoricity of the mathematical formula.[1]

Of course, this is in no sense a purely academic matter. The disinterest in history does not merely dominate modern social scientific thought and the analytic philosophy which serves it, or threaten the historian's right to existence.[2] In addition, individuals in everyday life do without historical consciousness. As Nietzsche put it, they remain "within the narrowest of horizons."[3]

However, this finding is not the result of a neutral sociology of education. Rather, as Adorno emphatically stressed, an overpowering tendency which is itself derived from history manifests itself in the loss of historical consciousness in countless individuals. The "shrinking of the consciousness of historical continuity," Adorno wrote, "is more than an aspect of decline—it is necessarily linked with the principle of progress in bourgeois society."[4] Adorno explains the alienation of contemporary consciousness from history with an economic-materialist analysis rather than, as is usually the case, allowing it to present itself as a scientific norm:

Bourgeois society is universally subjected to the law of exchange, of balanced calculations of "equals for equals" at the end of which literally nothing remains. Exchange is, according to its own essence, a timeless phenomenon, as are ratio and the operations of mathematics, which in their pure form exclude the aspect of time. Hence concrete time disappears from the sphere of industrial production, which now has little use for accumulated experience. Economists and sociologists such as Werner Sombart and Max Weber have assigned the principle of traditionalism to feudal society and that of rationality to bourgeois society. But this attribution implies no less than that memory, time, and recollection . . . are being liquidated as irrational residues. The fact that people divest themselves of the capacity for memory and breathlessly rush into accommodation with an eternal present reflects an objective developmental law.[5]

The contemporary discussion demonstrates that Adorno was justified in viewing the depressing atrophy of historical consciousness (which on a prescientific level emerges in the "repression" of the crimes of the recent past) as symptomatic of a general "weakening of the ego"[6] in the postliberal era. In *The Dialectic of Enlightenment*, Horkheimer and Adorno attempted to explain this phenomenon with an economic analysis. They argued that historical continuity and an undamaged subjectivity still capable of reflection belong together. From this perspective it is only logical that leading structuralist theorists combine a critique of traditional, chronologically oriented historical thinking with an equally harsh criticism of the concept of the unity and immanently historical nature of the ego. In so doing, they obliterate the epistemological subject-object problematic.[7]

As indispensable as it may be, a conscious working through of the past comprises only one side of historical consciousness. Truly "historical individuals," as the young Nietzsche called them, do not exhaust themselves in preserving, lamenting, or honoring earlier periods. Their "vision of the past turns them toward the future, . . . kindles the hope that justice will yet come and happiness is behind the mountain they are climbing."[8] They have understood how deeply past and future are intertwined with one another. They understand their own present in light of processes that have already run their course, and they struggle for a more human future. But in so doing—no one knew this better than Nietzsche—they think and act, in spite of their historical knowledge and cultivation, at bottom "unhistorically" because they think and act without regard for the existing state of affairs. Their intensive labor in history "does not serve pure knowledge but life."[9] This does not bother Nietzsche, for "man can only become man . . . by his power of transforming events into history."[10] For Nietzsche, the point is always to break through rigid and burdensome structures.

An approach to history which is hostile to history, in the dialectical sense presented in *The Use and Abuse of History*, and which serves "a powerful life-current of the developing culture" will never be able to claim that it is a pure "science" comparable to mathematics.[11] But it can, Nietzsche argues, free us from the false objectivity of thinglike, rigidified factuality merely waiting to be registered, a factuality which, in his view, as an opponent of positivism, "is always dull, at all times more like a calf than a god."[12] It is just those who are endowed with a historical, that is, theoretical, sense who are not apologists for what has already taken place and for its insignificant fluctuations. They resist, rather than drift along on, historical currents. They struggle against the "blind force of facts, the tyranny of the actual."[13]

Our temporal distance to Nietzsche's great utopian project allows us to evaluate the difficulties encountered by contemporary historical consciousness. An idea of history which rests on Marx and Marxism is not immune from these difficulties. The Marxist conception of history, just as that of its supposedly secular opponent, Nietzsche, is strongly oriented to the present.[14] It views the knowledge of the past and future as dependent on the "correct grasp of the present."[15] Marx is also related to Nietzsche in stressing the antihistorical moment within historical thinking. As he wrote in *The Eighteenth Brumaire of Louis Bonaparte*,

Men make their own history, but they do not make it just as they please; they do not make it under circumstances chosen by themselves, but under circumstances directly encountered, given and transmitted from the past. The tradition of all the dead generations weighs like a nightmare on the brain of the living.[16]

In a manner distinct from, yet indebted to, Hegel, Marx places the subjective-objective "double character" of the historical process in the center of his considerations. It is just this double character that has been recently challenged, particularly by authors who consider themselves to be Marxists. Hence Althusser, the founder of an interpretation of Marx inspired by structuralism, claims to be able to take from Marx's *Capital* the idea "that it is absolutely essential . . . to suppress every origin and every subject, and to say: what is absolute is the process without a subject, both in reality and in scientific knowledge."[17] Elsewhere, even more precisely, Althusser explains that "since Marx, we have known that the human subject, the economic, political, or philosophical ego is not the 'center' of history—and even, in opposition to the Philosophers of the Enlightenment and to Hegel, that history has no 'center' but possesses a structure which has no necessary 'center' except in ideological misrecognition."[18]

It does not necessarily follow from this that the Marx interpretation of the Althusser school must deny history completely. Rather it strives for a theory of transformation processes of social structures in which the methodological priority accorded to the synchronic over the diachronic inevitably means that questions concerning the content of historical experience are dealt with in a cursory manner or are devalued from the outset. What can remain in the way of a theory of history from an interpretation which has already characterized the question concerning the unified subject of historical movement as "ideological"?

The historian Reinhard Wittram has written that "nowhere . . . has history been accorded as much importance as in the thought of Karl Marx."[19] This is certainly correct. However, in view of the contemporary situation, this sentence has become a subject of controversy even among Marxists. The most recent attack on history, surpasses mere cultural pessimism. It is carried out with conceptual means which are not easily dismissed. Hence Althusser, intent on scientific rigor, advances a critique of the concept of "historical time" and of the role it plays in providing the foundation for the Hegelian and, ultimately, the Marxist dialectic as well.

This essay continues my own work in epistemology and the theory of history which has appeared in recent years.[20] I am aware that the structuralist polemic against the all-too-smooth linearity of a naive, evolutionist understanding of history, a view that was not at all alien to the Marxism of the Second International, contains moments of truth. Therefore the point is not to establish a simple antithesis between historical-dialectical and structuralist methods. Every metacritique of the Althusserian Marx-exegesis must simultaneously attempt to apply its productive results to itself. But even those who do not accept the thesis—which is fundamental for Althusser—that Marx's lifework presents two absolutely separate "problematics," an "ideological" one in the early writings and a "scientific" one in *Capital*,[21] will see how little one can speak of a "historicism" imprisoned by mere chronology in the work of the mature Marx.

In any case, the thesis which is being argued (in opposition to Althusser) in the following essay is that the "constructive" aspect of the method of *Capital* can be more adequately grounded in a *materialist interpretation* of Hegel. Insofar as I am attempting to defend the Hegelian heritage in Marx, I will do so by examining the role of the dialectic in *Capital*, referring primarily to Hegel's *Science of Logic* in the process. At many points the ensuing critique of Althusser turns into a positive presentation of Marx, from the material of political economy to the epistemology that is inseparable from it.

This essay should contribute to the epistemological reflection on materialist historical thought which has recently begun in various places and which constitutes an important task, not least of all in a political sense. In using the term *Historik* (theory of history), I am referring to Johann Gustav Droysen's well-known book, which he viewed—in a partially critical reception of Hegel—as a "scientific theory of history . . . as its encyclopedia and methodology."[22] Regardless of its obvious differences with Marxist materialism,[23] Droysen's work contains a great deal that is worth considering, especially today. Jörn Rüsen, a commentator on Droysen's work, stresses that in his *Historik*, Droysen sees in "politics, historical scholarship, and historical theory . . . equally significant moments of a single intention."[24] For Droysen, none of these three activities is, a priori, superior to the

other two. All rest on material history which, in turn, can be
unraveled only from the perspective of the present and its
needs. His conception of history seeks to link historical scholarship and politics together by uniting "historical knowing and
historical reality" at the point at which "the subject and object of
historical scholarship merge into one another, that is, on the
front of history taking place now or living in memory or antici-
pation."[25] This, in turn, points to a materialist element in Droysen's work, namely, that scientific rationality must enlighten
itself concerning the premethodological, social-practical presuppositions of its subject matter.[26] It was this which Horkheimer defined as constitutive of the transition from "traditional"
to "critical" theory. Who would wish to deny that Droysen's questions, mutatis mutandis, are also the questions of a Marxist *Historik*, or theory of history?

Droysen recognizes the relative appropriateness of describing
historical method apart from its contents. Ultimately, however,

such a separation of the formal and the substantive has only a
doctrinaire nature. . . . [It is] only a theoretical separation which
our mind must carry out in order to master the multiplicity of
the actual and changing [aspects of history]. As soon as we actually engage in historical research, it becomes evident . . . that
the substantive and the formal are always, to a large extent, in
relations of community and reciprocity to one another.[27]

From this follows Droysen's sentence (obviously inspired by Hegel): "The essence of historical method is *researching for the sake
of understanding*."[28] In spite of epistemological reservations,
method is determined "by the morphological character of its
material."[29] In other words, historical scholarship deals with,
and must adapt to, material that is always already structured.
However, in so doing it does not produce a "mirror image of the
present and the past . . . but rather a conception of them which
continuously expands, supplements, and corrects itself."[30] For
Droysen, an ego which is simply identical and atemporal is in-

conceivable. Rather, its "content" is always "a mediated, developed, that is, historical result."[31]

In contrast to subsequent usage of the word (as in Scheler), Droysen does not understand *Historik* to imply a speculative construction claiming total knowledge of world history. He is as suspicious of a "philosophy (or theology) of history" as of "a physics of the historical world."[32] Instead, like thinkers from Kant to Lukács and Sartre, he adheres to the principle—which has come under attack from the structuralists—that humanity, considered as a "general," continuously self-developing "ego," constitutes the "subject of history."[33] However, Droysen is careful not to determine the course of history in a dogmatic manner. "The *Historik* . . . must set itself the task of being an organon of historical thinking and research." It encompasses its "methodology . . . the systematization of the subject of historical research, and the topics under which the results of historical research are presented."[34]

According to Droysen, historical method is adequate to its task if it reflects the special nature of its material. Droysen, like Marx in his reference to Vico, emphasizes that in the strictest sense only that concerns us which "has been formed, stamped, and moved by the human mind and human hand."[35] In relation to these historical products, he continues, "We are and feel ourselves to be essentially similar and in relations of reciprocity."[36] Although Droysen does not employ a dialectical terminology, considerations such as these are of a dialectical nature. The subject-object structure of the historical elevates the researcher above abstract alternatives. Simultaneously, he must proceed synthetically and analytically, inductively and deductively. The same holds true for the relation between the part and the whole: they reciprocally illuminate one another. The individual empirical finding becomes an individual "totality in itself,"[37] only in a comprehensible context of a more encompassing social whole. It would, however, be wrong to absolutize the latter.

In spite of their shortcomings, the relevance of Droysen's lectures on historical methodology for the reflection of Marxist materialism on itself derives not only from the above-mentioned issues in the contemporary theory of history but also from historical discussions of these issues. I shall briefly recall these discussions, since they lead to the question of the object-domain of a Marxist historical method.

In that it is related to the young Dilthey's "critique of historical reason," Droysen's undertaking belongs to the post-Idealist period. As a consequence of the much-discussed collapse of Hegelian speculation, "historical understanding" emerged as a new type of thought. Consequently questions in the vaguely demarcated zone lying between dogmatic historical metaphysics, the research practice of individual historical disciplines, and contemporary political history became acute. In addition, the human sciences (*Geisteswissenschaften*), which had developed in the first half of the nineteenth century, stood in need of a foundation that would distinguish them methodologically from the natural sciences.

Dilthey, the philosopher of life (*Lebensphilosoph*), tried to offer to the human sciences an atemporal, psychologically and anthropologically grounded model combined with a limitless relativism. Marxist criticism demonstrated how fragile and antinomic this effort must be.[38]

Marx and Engels were among the authors who contributed to the breakthrough of historical thinking in the last century. They faced the difficult question of how, out of the complex, infinitely rich reality of history, a theoretical pattern could emerge that we call "history." The new "science of history,"[39] which they inaugurated in the 1840s and endowed with universal significance, diverged from the academic historicism of the post-Hegelian period in three essential ways.

1. It opposed all tendencies which postulated an absolute difference, or even contradiction, between nature and history, and

thus between the modes of knowing them. Rather, according to Marx and Engels, both nature and history belong to the same world, one whose cognitive (and also increasingly actual) unity is established by collective praxis. "The history of nature and the history of men are dependent on each other so long as men exist."[40] Hence they argued that the unity of man and nature was not—as previous materialism had assumed—of a merely genetic nature but "has always existed in industry and has existed in varying forms in every epoch."[41] Against Feuerbach, Marx and Engels argue that he did not see

that the sensuous world . . . is not a thing given direct from all eternity, remaining ever the same, but the product . . . of the state of society, . . . a historical product, the result of the activity of a whole succession of generations, each standing on the shoulders of the preceding one. . . . Even objects of the simplest "sensuous certainty" are only given him through social development, industry, and commercial intercourse.[42]

These considerations are important for the theory of history because they demonstrate that Marx and Engels do not indulge in a "realism of historical method."[43] On the contrary, they expressly object to "so-called *objective* historiography" which attempts "to treat historical relations separately from activity."[44]

It should be stressed immediately that "activity," in this sense, refers not only to the social life-process, which presents itself to the individual as a completed immediacy, but also, and just as much, to the (in the strict sense of the word) *critical* activity of the scholar who traces the multiple natural-historical and social-historical mediations of his empirical findings. The objectively mediated nature of this material (something of which everyday thinking remains unconscious) corresponds to the theoretical task of subordinating "the flatly obvious, the sensuous *appearance*, to the sensuous reality established by detailed investigation of the sensuous facts."[45] According to Marx and Engels, it was not wrong for Feuerbach to distinguish the surface from the essence of things, but he "cannot in the last resort cope with the sensuous world except by looking at it with the 'eyes,' that is, through the 'spectacles,' of the philosopher."[46]

In fact, with the sober description of the material processes of production, "a self-sufficient philosophy loses its medium of existence."[47] For now, Marx and Engels argue, it becomes possible to uncover the "real basis," that at which metaphysical concepts such as "substance" and "human essence" aim: "the sum of productive forces, capital funds, and social forms of intercourse, which every individual and every generation finds in existence as something given."[48] In other words, they do not dismiss speculation as mere nonsense but arrive at its real content. Speculation enters into the conceptual apparatus of their materialist research and serves "to facilitate the arrangement of historical material, [and] to indicate the sequence of its separate strata."[49] It is clear that Marx and Engels were anything but methodologically naive. They did not, as a consequence of their break with Idealism, prescribe a restricted positivity. On the contrary, it was from Hegel that they knew how important it was to give voice to the object. Intellectually unmastered history amounts, in their words, to a "collection of dead facts."[50] By contrast, the historian working within a materialist framework must be intent on grasping the object, that is, on representing it in "its totality."[51]

2. A further difference (related to this discussion) between the materialist theory of history and bourgeois historicism is that the former destroys the notion that there is a purely immanent, an ideal, course of events.

It is noteworthy that it was precisely the idealist, Hegel, who, with his idea that *only the whole* spirit has a "real history,"[52] pointed the way toward a materialist critique of the "history of ideas" (*Geistesgeschichte*), viewed as the sum total of specialized and isolated partial histories. As Hegel wrote in *The Phenomenology of Mind*, "It is only spirit in its entirety that is in time, and the shapes assumed, which are specific embodiments of the whole of spirit as such, present themselves in a sequence one after the other. For it is only the whole which properly has reality."[53]

Starting from the Hegelian idea of the totality, Marx and Engels developed their theory of the historical process as constituting a lawful sequence of economic formations of society. In their view, the "relations of production" were to be conceived structurally rather than as a determining "factor" (alongside other, less important factors). The structure which they take on at different times transforms an epoch into a concrete, ascertainable totality. It is only the totality which has a history accessible to a unified theory:

The phantoms formed in the brains of men are also, necessarily, sublimates of their material life-premises. Morality, religion, metaphysics, and all the rest of ideology as well as the forms of consciousness corresponding to these, thus no longer retain the semblance of independence. They have no history, no development; but men developing their material production and their material intercourse alter along with this their actual world, also their thinking and the products of their thinking.[54]

The impossibility of grounding history anthropologically follows from this argument. If, as Marx and Engels hold, there is "in addition to the spirit of the real, materially evolved individuals," no "separate spirit," the historical process does not express what can be interpreted as a continuous, unified "meaning."[55] Human beings as well as their culture succumb to radical transitoriness.[56]

In order to clarify the matter more clearly, let us return to the problematic concept of *Geistesgeschichte*. Dilthey, of course, speaks of the world of objective spirit that is always already given. However, what is decisive for him remains the idea that this world can be explained only psychologically, that is, through the self-verification of individual "experience." He grounds the unity of experience in the "structural connections of the life of the soul,"[57] a phenomenon behind which, in Dilthey's view, we cannot investigate further. He continues, "Because the systems of culture . . . have emerged from the living connections of the human soul, they can be understood only on the basis of this soul. Psychic facts comprise the most important elements of cultural systems. Hence they cannot be understood without psychological analysis."[58]

If, for Dilthey, psychology conceived in this sense becomes an indispensable auxiliary discipline to history, he seeks on the other hand, to derive from the objectivity of history that with which psychology is to concern itself. For example, he writes that "it is only in history, never in introspection, that the individual attains self-recognition."[59] Indeed Dilthey, just like contemporary structuralists, holds that even the question of traditional philosophy of history—whether the historical process has an immanent "goal" or "overall direction"—is "completely one-sided."[60] History, he maintains, proceeds less in a linear-progressive manner than in "separate consequences that are related to one another."[61] According to Dilthey, it is in these consequences, "which are always present," that "the manifest meaning of history . . . [must] be sought moving from the structure of the individual life up to the final, most all-encompassing unity: it is the meaning which history has at every place and point in time, which determined past development, and to which the future will be subjected."[62] Dilthey writes that whoever investigates the structure of cultural spheres must demonstrate these "regularities in the structure of the historical world."[63] Thus for Dilthey, the question concerning a—developing—absolute in history is an unscientific and hence idle one.

It is in this manner that Dilthey's radical, historical thinking (he himself characterizes the "consciousness . . . of the finiteness of every social condition" as the "last step in the liberation of individuals")[64] terminates in a static ontology which logically precedes actual events. Because he is unable dialectically to overcome the antinomy between inescapable relativity and a claim to objective truth, he makes do with the Idealist assumption that all change takes place "within the uniformities of human nature." He points to "particularizations"[65] which the historian must study: "On the basis of the uniformity of processes which run through all individuals, individuality, levels of differentiations between individualities, affinities, types, etc., emerge, all of which constitute the object of comparative psychology."[66]

Dilthey, convinced that "the uniform [is] the foundation of individuation,"[67] views the great cultural periods as transient forms of expression of something unchanging. That is, over centuries the homogeneous essence of individuals fans out toward its different aspects. According to Dilthey, what is originally found in every person emerges in heightened form in the "representative personalities" in whom the "cultural constitution of a whole epoch"[68] is expressed: "Human races, nations, social classes, occupational forms, historical levels—all are . . . demarcations of individual differentiations within a uniform human nature,"[69] which finds a specific expression in every era.

The dubious nature of conceiving human essence in this manner is clear. Dilthey's metaphysics raises to the level of (differentiating) aspects of the objectivations—of psychologically interpreted—"life," what are in fact utterly distinct, natural, social-economic, and generally historical circumstances with which an epochal constellation of "cultural systems" is associated.

It is difficult to understand how the cultural phenomena, not to mention the unity, of an epoch rest on a structure of the soul which in each case manifests one aspect of the whole nature of human beings. (In contrast to Hegel, Dilthey did not necessarily evaluate such manifestations as signs of progress.) In view of the manifestly antagonistic course of history, it is advisable to speak with caution about such an exceedingly fragile totality.

Furthermore, at all levels of the interaction of socially organized individuals, this historical process connects them to both human and nonhuman external nature. Consequently there is no "pure" human essence that comes to expression in this process and that would be accessible to a "psychology of understanding." Neither a particular period nor a sequence of stages can be grasped on the basis of, in Horkheimer's words, "the unified life of the soul of a universal human nature."[70] According to Horkheimer, "When history is divided up in accordance with the different modes in which the life process of . . . society takes place, it is economic, not psychological, categories, which are the fundamental ones."[71]

3. Historical materialism distinguishes itself from bourgeois historiography through its conception of "world history." Whereas traditional textbooks understand world and universal history— terms that are often used promiscuously—as the "effort to attain a total view of the whole historical process since the beginnings of human culture,"[72] for Marx and Engels the concept had additional theoretical connotations.

The following note, as concise as it is substantive, appears in the *Contribution to the Critique of Political Economy* of 1857: "World history has not always existed; history as world history is a result."[73] For Marx it is crucial that "the concept of progress . . . not be grasped in the usual abstractness."[74] In the 1850s, as he turned his attention to an almost overwhelming amount of social-historical material (and thus began preliminary work on *Capital*), he became aware of the uselessness of a rigid linear schema of successive historical stages. Marx is concerned not only with "the uneven development of material production relative to, for example, artistic production" but also with the considerable disproportions and cleavages that he confronts "within practical-social relations themselves."[75] For example, Marx asks how one can explain the fact that the modern relations of production, considered as legal relations, remain within the confines of Roman law, which, in turn, presupposes a completely different economy. This is a difficult question, one which caused Marx to pay attention to the complex dialectic of chance and necessity. His texts from this period testify to the care with which he proceeded on this point.

The most important result of Marx's comprehensive historical studies, studies which—and this is not always recognized today—constitute, and to that extent belong to, the material foundation of his whole political-economic theory, is his insight into the radical historicization of history (*Vergeschichtlichung der Geschichte*) that occurs with the "development" and "existence" of capitalist production. History becomes world history to the extent to which individuals emerge from the naturalness of pre-bourgeois groups and communities and live in the context of relationships which are produced rather than given:

Thus capital creates the bourgeois society and the universal appropriation of nature as well as the social bond itself by members of society. Hence the great civilizing influence of capital; its production of a stage of society in comparison to which all earlier ones appear as mere local developments of humanity and as native idolatry. . . . In accordance with this tendency, capital drives beyond national barriers and prejudices as well as traditional, confined, complacent, encrusted satisfactions of present needs and the reproduction of old ways of life. It . . . tears down all the barriers that hem in the development and exchange of natural and mental forces.[76]

Marx would not have been the dialectical thinker he was had he been content with merely celebrating the emancipatory, epoch-making role of capital. Indeed when speaking of the human content of the wealth developed in the modern world, Marx never forgets to stress its "narrow bourgeois form"[77] and to insist on the necessity of transcending this form. In the *Grundrisse* he returns to the central theme of the *Economic and Philosophical Manuscripts* (1844) when he emphasizes that under existing relationships, "the complete working out of the human content [must appear] as a complete emptying out [*Entleerung*], this universal objectification as total alienation, and the tearing down of all limited, one-sided aims as sacrifice of the human end in itself to an entirely external end."[78]

Thus the characteristic reversal of the positive into the negative is not merely an appearance present in the consciousness of individuals. Rather it is a real process, expanded and repeated daily in the growth of "the monstrous objective power which social labor itself erected opposite itself as one of its moments."[79] The necessity of this process is historical, not absolute. Only when living labor in its immediate form no longer emerges as an isolated phenomenon, only with the overcoming of its character

as merely internal . . . or merely external, with the positing of the activity of individuals as immediately general or social activity, [are] the objective moments of production stripped of this form of alienation; they are thereby posited as property, as the organic social body within which individuals reproduce themselves as individuals, but as social individuals.[80]

These are formulations which clearly outline the specifically historical-philosophical aspects of Marx's historical thinking. In them, the unity of the whole of Marx's intentions is evident (something that escapes the scientistically narrowed outlook of the structuralists). From the earliest to the most mature writings, Marx's work is defined by the idea of the "free social individual,"[81] an idea which cannot be evaluated simply on the basis of academic criteria taken directly from any single academic discipline but should be understood as something mediated in conjunction with the evolution of social wealth. For what does bourgeois particularity set free other than "the universality of needs, capacities, pleasures, productive forces of individuals created through universal exchange"?[82] In Marx's view, the ideal of the generally human can cease to be an empty phrase and become reality as a result of the "absolute working out [of] the creative potentialities"[83] of all individuals. For Marx, the idea of wealth unleashed means that the "totality of development" would be elevated to an "end in itself" and that it could not be subordinated to a "predetermined yardstick." In his view, liberated humanity does not yearn "to remain something that it has become" but rather resides "in the absolute movement of becoming."[84]

In 1844, Marx had already written, "Reason has always existed but not always in a rational form. Hence the critic can take his cue from every existing form of theoretical and practical consciousness, and from this ideal and final goal implicit in the actual forms of existing reality he can deduce a true reality."[85] Here Marx sketches the materialist basis of his revolutionary humanism. By confronting a restricted instrumental reason with its "rational form," and "existing reality" with a "true reality," Marx stresses the necessity of deriving the shape of the future from a material analysis of the present rather than attempting to do so with mere constructs. This is precisely the decisive theme of the *Grundrisse*. As Marx wrote,

The most extreme form of alienation wherein labor appears in the relation of capital and wage labor [and] productive activity appears in relation to its own conditions and its own product [is a] necessary point of transition [because] in itself, in a still only inverted form turned on its head, [the alienated condition contains] the dissolution of all limited presuppositions of production. [It creates its, that is, production's] unconditional presuppositions . . . and therewith the material conditions for the total, universal development of the productive powers of the individual.[86]

Marx's comments, in the well-known passage on the world-historical foundations of the "realm of freedom"[87] in volume 3 of *Capital*, correspond to the view expressed above.

These passages should make it clear that the philosophy of history constitutes only one—albeit indispensable—aspect of Marx's thinking about history. It consists of more of a radical humanistic impulse which gladly embraces and grows out of substantive investigations than of a doctrinaire developmental schema. Marx, in the famous (later canonized) foreword to *A Contribution to the Critique of Political Economy*, explicitly referred to his theory that "the Asiatic, ancient, feudal, and modern bourgeois modes of production may be designated as epochs marking progress in the economic development of society"[88] as the "guiding principle"[89] of his studies. And in 1877 he felt compelled—on political grounds—to defend his "historical sketch of the emergence of capitalism in Western Europe"[90] (a reference to chapter 24 in the first volume of *Capital*) against a Russian author who had transformed it into a "historical-philosophical theory of a general developmental path which is prescribed as a fate for all peoples regardless of their historical conditions."[91] In Marx's view, such a "universal key" to history is mistaken. "Its great merit," he writes, "consists in being suprahistorical."[92] Marx the historian was not outwitted by Marx the historical theorist or politician. He combines an intellectual breadth, which keeps him away from surface description, with a respect for facts, which are often first established as facts per se only on the basis of theory.

I have now offered, in its material-historical aspects, a rough outline of the domain of a Marxist historical method. This domain encompasses, in Droysen's terms, mutatis mutandis, first of all a *Methodik*, that is, a set of reflections on history of a philosophical, theoretical, historiographical, and even political nature. Because the demarcation lines between these objectively conditioned modes of viewing history are only relative, it does not follow that we may neglect their differences. What holds true for the theory of dialectical materialism as a whole also applies to historical method and its construction, namely, that it is neither an undifferentiated unity[93] nor a sum of unrelated isolated disciplines.

The above should be kept in mind in order to prevent the possible misunderstanding that my intention in this work is purely academic and removed from the substantive problems of Marxism (which are simultaneously problems of our time). On the contrary, in putting forth the concept of a Marxist historical method (*marxistischen Historik*), I think I am able to focus general attention on a complex of problems whose contemporary significance I emphasized at the outset. In so doing I would like to contribute to, as the young Lukács put it, grasping the present as history.

This book deals primarily with an object that Droysen (who, unlike Dilthey, was certainly not a precursor of structuralist historical thinking) would have attributed to the areas of "systematic" and "topic." Owing to its polemical tack, however, the introductory part deals relatively extensively with questions concerning material rather than formalized history.

As the state of the discussion, especially in France, demonstrates, Barthes was right when in 1966 he conjectured that in the future the "main resistance to structuralism" would probably come from Marxists and that this resistance would "center on the concept of history rather than the concept of structure."[94] Whereas interpreters of Marx had hitherto asserted that both concepts existed in a "dialectical unity" (usually discussed under the heading "relation of the logical to the historical"), this often only formal statement no longer sufficed. To the extent that structuralist thinking emigrated from linguistics into the social sciences and then established a preserve there, an important reconsideration was instituted in Marxism—above all in French Marxism: history (diachrony) and structure (synchrony) moved far apart from one another. At the very least, their hitherto merely asserted unity was rendered problematic. Thus Marx's *Capital* moved toward the center of heated debates between Althusser and his students, on the one hand, and well-known authors such as Sartre, Lefebvre, and Garaudy, on the other.

This book picks up the threads of this still-uncompleted discussion, one which I have been following for a long time. When the representatives of the Althusser school criticize the "historicist" and "humanistic" interpretation of Marx, they have in mind Gramsci, above all. They reject his identification of philosophical theory with history and the writing of history just as vehemently as they themselves place *Capital* as a "pure theoretical work" in unmediated contradiction to "concrete history."[95] This book weighs the rights and wrongs of Gramsci's and Althusser's respective positions. In addition, it interprets the works of the mature Marx against the background of his materialist Hegel reception. As a result, the previously insufficiently explained role that the Hegelian "system," with its complex relationship to the historical process, played in Marx's critique of political economy will become clear. This recourse to Hegel is indispensable insofar as it allows us to escape from the circle of a knowable structure without history and an unknowable history without structure.

Parts of this book were delivered as lectures in January 1970 at the University of Heidelberg, and in June 1971 at the Ulmer Institut für Umweltplanung (Ulm Institute for Environmental Planning), at the University of Tübingen, and at the Kölner Konferenz für Kunsttheorie (Cologne Conference on the Theory of Art). I thank participants in the discussions for their criticisms and suggestions.

Frankfurt, September 1971

Notes

1. Herbert Lüthy, *Die Mathematisierung der Sozialwissenschaften* (Zurich, 1970), pp. 28, 31, 37. Also see Lüthy's *Wozu Geschichte?* (Zurich, 1969), p. 44. On the aspect of this methodological repression of history which concerns the critique of language and ideology, see Herbert Marcuse, *One-Dimensional Man* (Boston, 1964).

2. Concerning this problem, see the instructive study by Reinhard Wittram, *Anspruch und Fragwürdigkeit der Geschichte: Sechs Vorlesungen zur Methodik der Geschichtswissenschaft und zur Ortsbestimmung der Historie* (Göttingen, 1969).

3. Friedrich Nietzsche, *The Use and Abuse of History*, trans. Adrian Collins (Indianapolis, 1949), p. 8.

4. Theodor W. Adorno, "Was bedeutet: Aufarbeitung der Vergangenheit," in *Erziehung zur Mündigkeit* (Frankfurt am Main, 1970), p. 13.

5. Ibid., p. 13.

6. Ibid. Hegel, in *The Philosophy of Nature*, sec. 258, also equates the continuously flowing time of "perceived mere becoming" (*angeschaute blosse Werden*) with the "self-identical ego of pure self-consciousness" (*Ich=Ich des reinen Selbstbewusstseins*).

7. When Althusser interprets Marx's theory as "theoretical" antihistoricism and antihumanism, each of these aspects conditions and presupposes the other. Even he—although negatively—picks up the threads of Hegel's insight in *The Phenomenology of Mind* according to which epistemology and theory of history are reflected in one another.

Lévi-Strauss, in whose well-known works the *taedium historiae* is especially evident, denies to historical scholarship the right to be preferred to other forms of knowledge. On this see his critical discussion of Sartre's *Critique of Dialectical Reason* in the last chapter of *The Savage Mind* (Chicago, 1966). Lévi-Strauss views the "totalizing continuity of the self . . . to be an illusion sustained by the demands of social life. . . . And as we believe that we apprehend the trend of our personal history as a continuous change, historical knowledge appears to confirm the evidence of inner sense" (ibid., p. 256). The historian (just as little as Sartre's philosophy) is not content with describing beings to us from the outside. "It appears to reestablish our connection, outside ourselves, with the very essence of change" (ibid.). However, according to Lévi-Strauss, this does not overcome the difficulty because the concept of the actual occurrence, of the "historical fact," remains problematic. "Each episode in a revolution or a war resolves itself into a multitude of individual psychic movements. Each of these movements is the translation of unconscious development, and these resolve themselves into cerebral, hormonal, or nervous phenomena, which themselves have reference to the physical or chemical order" (ibid., p. 257). Lévi-Strauss's crass naturalistic reductions, in which nothing of history remains, lead into the "abstract materialism of natural science, a materialism which excludes the *historical process*" and which Marx criticized in in *Capital* (vol. 1, trans. Ben Fowkes; New York, 1977, p. 494, emphasis in original). Even one who does not accept an absolute difference between natural and human history will agree with Marx against Lévi-Strauss that the facts of the latter are "more" given than mere facts of nature *because we have made them* (ibid., p. 493). It is true that the historian must proceed through abstraction and selection, and in researching individual facts always stands "under the threat of an infinite regress" (Lévi-Strauss, *The Savage Mind*, p. 257). However, such problems need not have the ruinous consequences which the structuralists assume they must. It goes without saying that this problematic can only be mentioned here. It cannot be adequately and fully discussed.

8. Nietzsche, *The Use and Abuse of History*, p. 10.

9. Ibid.

10. Ibid., p. 8.

11. Ibid., p. 12.

12. Ibid., p. 53.

13. Ibid., p. 54.

14. Modern historians such as Reinhard Wittram leave no doubt that the historian's "present" has an "important function in historical knowledge." See his *Das Interesse an der Geschichte: Zwölf Vorlesungen über Fragen des zeitgenössischen Geschichtsverständnisses* (Göttingen, 1958), p. 10.

15. Karl Marx, *Grundrisse: Foundations of the Critique of Political Economy*, trans. Martin Nicolaus (Middlesex, England, and Baltimore, Md., 1973), p. 461.

16. Karl Marx, *The Eighteenth Brumaire of Louis Bonaparte*, in *Karl Marx and Friedrich Engels: Selected Works* (New York, 1968), p. 97.

17. Louis Althusser, *Lenin and Philosophy and Other Essays*, trans. Ben Brewster (London, 1971), p. 119.

18. Ibid., p. 201.

19. Wittram, *Anspruch und Fragwürdigkeit der Geschichte*, p. 23.

20. See Alfred Schmidt, "Der strukturalistische Angriff auf die Geschichte," pp. 194–265, in *Beiträge zur marxistischen Erkenntnistheorie*, ed. Alfred Schmidt (Frankfurt am Main, 1969).

21. Louis Althusser, *For Marx*, trans. Ben Brewster (New York, 1970), p. 13.

22. Johann Gustav Droysen, *Historik: Vorlesungen über Enzyklopädie und Methodol-*

ogie der Geschichte, ed. Rudolf Hubner (Munich, 1967), p. 377. On Droysen see the two works by Jörn Rüsen, *Begriffene Geschichte: Geschichte und Begründung der Geschichtstheorie J.G. Droysens* (Paderborn, 1969), and "Politisches Denken und Geschichtswissenschaft bei J.G. Droysen," in *Politische Ideologien und nationalstaatliche Ordnung* (Munich and Vienna, 1968). Rüsen's solid and penetrating studies are of great interest for the present work. In the latter essay mentioned above, Rüsen shows that in Droysen's work there is "a unity of politics and historical scholarship which is typical for the epoch of the bourgeois revolution in Germany. History as the object of historical research is at the same time, for Droysen, a spur to political practice whose theoretical guidelines emerge from scientific investigation of the heritage and contemporary presence of the past" (p. 171). "If history is supposed to be constitutive for the self-understanding of the present at the point at which it is translated into practice, then the abstract alternative of a depoliticized historical scholarship, on the one hand, and a dehistoricized politics, on the other, must be abandoned" (ibid.). According to Rüsen, Droysen's work is a plea for historical scholarship "which has been made painfully aware of the loss of its practical dimension" to assert once again "its political claim" (ibid.). Also important in this connection is Rüsen's remark on the dubious nature of interpretations of Droysen which see him "as the precursor of a theory of history . . . that is oriented less to historical contents than to the forms of knowing them and that therefore abandons any explicit connection with contemporary history. Such an interpretation depoliticizes Droysen's theory of history (*Historik*). Once formalized into the conceptual apparatus of a historical hermeneutic and of historical event-structures, the theory, as a theory of historicity, loses its foundation in contemporary history" (ibid., p. 175). Of course, Rüsen adds that it would be just as mistaken "to subsume Droysen's work under the rubric of the politicization of historical scholarship centered on the nation-state. . . . For the inseparable connection between historical description, politics, and theory in Droysen's work is the fruit of an insight into a . . . development whose consequences directly determine the contemporary discussion of the problem of history" (*Begriffene Geschichte*, p. 62).

23. For example, Droysen's *Historik* takes as its point of departure (see pp. 13, 19) a dichotomy—which formulated in this way has become untenable—between nature and history: "Natural history (*Naturgeschichte*) is only *vel quasi* history. In the eminent sense, history is only history of the ethical cosmos, history of the human world." Certainly, in a short passage (sec. 51), Droysen mentions that the "intervention of the human hand into the life of nature and its transformation . . . has a genuinely historical character." But he does not draw the necessary consequences from this insight. The fact that the nature which has been worked over and the social forms of its appropriation—forms that, in turn, imply particular class relations—enter into the material substance of history as decisive moments remains undiscussed.

24. Rüsen, *Politisches Denken und Geschichtswissenschaft bei J.G. Droysen*, p. 174.

25. Ibid., p. 175.

26. Cf. ibid., p. 174.

27. Droysen, *Historik*, p. 189.

28. Ibid., p. 328 (emphasis in original).

29. Ibid.; see also p. 415 where Droysen rejects epistemological subjectivism.

30. Ibid., p. 7; see also p. 345.

31. Ibid., p. 332.

32. Ibid., p. 331.

33. Ibid., p. 267.

34. Ibid., p. 331. Droysen explains these three aspects of his *Historik* on pp. 332–366.

35. Ibid., p. 328.

36. Ibid., p. 329.

37. Ibid.

38. Cf. George Lukács, *Die Zerstörung der Vernunft* (Berlin, 1954), p. 341. Lukács's polemic against *Lebensphilosophie* may well hit an important aspect of the highly complicated work of Dilthey. However, the studies by Gorsen, Habermas, and Lieber demonstrate that Lukács's critique did not settle the matter. Manfred Riedel's essay, "Das erkenntniskritische Motiv in Diltheys Theorie der Geisteswissenschaften" points for this to historical parallels to Feuerbach, Marx, and Nietzsche that have not yet received much attention. In *Hermeneutik und Dialektik I*, ed. Rüdiger Bubner, Konrad Cramer, and Reiner Wiehl (Tübingen, 1979), pp. 233–255.

39. Karl Marx and Friedrich Engels, *The German Ideology*, vol. 5 of *Karl Marx and Friedrich Engels: Collected Works* (New York, 1976), p. 28.

40. Ibid.

41. Ibid., p. 39.

42. Ibid.

43. George Simmel understood this as the historiographical counterpart to this naive realism in the knowledge of nature. In his book *Die Probleme der Geschichtsphilosophie* (Munich and Leipzig, 1922), p. 54, Simmel wrote, "Historical method

is always given the task of allowing us to see things 'as they really were.' In contrast to this view, one must make it clear that every act of cognition is a translation of the immediately given into a new language, which has its own forms, categories, and demands. As the facts . . . enter into the realm of science, they must answer certain questions which are never put to them in reality. In order to satisfy the needs of knowledge, they receive an ordering scheme . . . which is, as it were, over the head of reality and which creates a new structure out of them."

44. Marx and Engels, *The German Ideology*, p. 55 (emphasis in original).

45. Ibid., p. 39.

46. Ibid., p. 37.

47. Ibid.

48. Ibid., p. 54.

49. Ibid., p. 37.

50. Ibid.

51. Ibid., p. 54.

52. George Lukács, *Der junge Hegel* (Berlin, 1954), p. 533 (emphasis in original). Also see George Lukács, *The Young Hegel*, trans. Rodney Livingstone, pt. IV (Cambridge, Mass., 1975).

53. G. W. F. Hegel, *The Phenomenology of the Mind*, trans. J. B. Baillie (New York, 1967), p. 49.

54. Marx and Engels, *The German Ideology*, pp. 36–37.

55. Ibid., p. 36.

56. Horkheimer's Marx interpretation in the *Zeitschrift für Sozialforschung* stressed the undeniable antimetaphysical, even nihilistic, moment in historical materialism. With interpreters such as Bloch or Lukács, this aspect of historical materialism is less in evidence because they adhere to the human species as the general subject of history. This humanistic motif also appears in the work of the mature Marx.

57. Wilhelm Dilthey, *Gesammelte Schriften*, vol. 5, ed. Bernhard Groethuysen (Stuttgart, 1957), p. 237.

58. Ibid., p. 147.

59. Dilthey, *Gesammelte Schriften*, vol. 7 (Stuttgart, 1958), p. 279.

60. Ibid., p. 172.

61. Ibid.; see also p. 307 where Dilthey directly challenges the idea that "in their concurrence and succession . . . historical events . . . have the means of deducing either a causal nexus connecting them, or laws of development governing them, or a progress or development that takes place in and through them." Today structural historians argue no differently.

62. Ibid.

63. Ibid., p. 173.

64. Ibid., p. 290.

65. Ibid., 5:225 (emphasis in original).

66. Ibid., p. 241.

67. Ibid., p. 268.

68. Ibid., p. 236.

69. Ibid.

70. Max Horkheimer, "Geschichte und Psychologie," in *Kritische Theorie*, vol. 1, ed. Alfred Schmidt (Frankfurt am Main, 1968), p. 29. Cf. Marx and Engels, *The German Ideology*, p. 61, on the critique of the idealist-anthropological belief "that all the relations of men can be derived from the concept of man, man as conceived, the essence of man, Man."

71. Ibid., p. 18.

72. Wolfgang Mommsen, "Universalgeschichte," in *Das Fischer Lexikon 24, Geschichte*, ed. Waldemar Besson (Frankfurt am Main, 1961), p. 328. Mommsen's definition is typical for many authors. On Marx he writes, "In spite of the force with which Marx, even more so than Hegel, constructed history according to a priori principles, his theory directed thinking on universal history in wholly new paths." However, Mommsen does not elaborate on what these paths were.

73. Karl Marx, *Grundrisse*, p. 109. [The *Introduction to the Critique of Political Economy* is the introduction to Marx's *Grundrisse*. It has also been published as *A Contribution to the Critique of Political Economy*, trans. S. W. Ryazanskaya, ed. with introduction by Maurice Dobb (London and New York, 1971). All quotations in this work are taken from Martin Nicolaus's translation of the *Grundrisse*.]

74. Ibid.

75. Ibid.

76. Marx, *Grundrisse*, pp. 409–410 (emphasis in original). Here Marx again takes up important motifs of his early writings, in particular *The German Ideology* and *The Communist Manifesto*.

77. Ibid., p. 488.

78. Ibid.; see also pp. 295–296, 415.

79. Ibid., p. 832.

80. Ibid. (emphasis in original).

81. Ibid.; cf. pp. 196–197.

82. Ibid., p. 488.

83. Ibid.

84. Ibid. (emphasis in original).

85. *Karl Marx and Frederick Engels: Collected Works*, vol. 1: *Early Writings*, trans. Rodney Livingstone (New York, 1975), p. 208 (emphasis in original).

86. Marx, *Grundrisse*, p. 515.

87. Karl Marx, *Capital*, vol. 3 (Moscow, 1962), pp. 842–845.

88. Marx, *Contribution to the Critique of Political Economy*, p. 21.

89. Ibid., p. 20.

90. "Marx an die Redaktion der 'Vaterländischen Blätter,' November 1877," in Marx/Engels, *Ausgewählte Briefe* (Berlin, 1953), p. 371.

91. Ibid.

92. Ibid.

93. In Marxism's period of decay, its rigidification into a closed ideology deadened to its own content was all too evidently revealed in conceptually unproven "transitions" from one plane of argumentation to another.

94. Roland Barthes, "Die strukturalistische Tätigkeit," *Kursbuch 5*, ed. Hans Magnus Enzensberger (Frankfurt am Main, 1966), p. 190.

95. Cf. Louis Althusser, "Wie sollen wir *Das Kapital* lesen?" trans. from an article in *Humanité*, March 21, 1969, p. 3. [No date and place of publication.]

History and Structure

Science as the Conscious Product of Historical Movement

In view of recent efforts to narrow or even deny the role of the historical in the thinking of Marx and Engels,[1] it should be recalled that at every stage of their development they saw in world history a decisive theme. *The German Ideology*, a work of fundamental importance for Marx's subsequent conceptions, contains a sentence whose importance cannot be overemphasized: "We know only a single science, the science of history."[2] In substance, Marx and Engels never moved away from this view. The new science, a product of the bourgeois world in general, and of the collapse of speculative idealism in particular, fundamentally transformed the concept of history. They wrote that it "ceases to be a collection of dead facts, as it is with the empiricists, or an imagined activity of an imagined subject, as with the idealists."[3] Now its "earthly basis"[4] is recognized. This recognition brings with it the insight, derived from the critique of ideology, that "formations of ideas" that were previously held to be autonomous are in fact separated, alienated moments of material praxis and therefore "cannot be dissolved by mental criticism ... but only by the practical overthrow of the actual social relations"[5] which give rise to them.

Soon after, from the perspective of political organization, the founder of dialectical materialism returned to the relation of the new science to history. In *The Poverty of Philosophy* Marx argues that it is the level of economic development of society which determines whether the literary representatives of the proletariat come forward as eccentric utopians or genuine revolutionaries. He argues that as long as the working class, in consequence of underdevelopment of the productive forces, has not constituted itself politically, that is, "as a class for itself,"[6] its advocates will "improvise systems . . . and seek science in their minds." By contrast, in the context of more advanced relationships, the critics have only "to take note of what is happening before their eyes and to become its mouthpiece." By beginning to grasp the "subversive side" of the negativity of existing relations, the science of these critics "which is produced by historical movement . . . has ceased to be doctrinaire and has become revolutionary."[7]

It is not valid, writes Marx, the mature economic analyst, to create science on the basis of a priori principles rather than on "the critical knowledge of the historical movement," which generates "the material conditions of emancipation."[8] This interest in the present as sedimented and still-to-be-formed history is constitutive for the Marxist idea of a revolutionary science. It is pervasive in Marx's *Capital*, a work with whose detailed interpretation Russian Marxism begins in a theoretical (and practical) sense. As Marx writes, it is "the ultimate aim of this work to reveal the economic law of motion of modern society."[9] Marx attaches the utmost importance to the idea that the dialectical method proceeds simultaneously in a structural-analytic and a historical manner. In his words, "It includes in its positive understanding of what exists a simultaneous recognition of its negation, its inevitable destruction."[10]

Of course, these ideas, as familiar as they are indispensable, cause epistemological difficulties, of which Marx and Engels were well aware. Because of their contemporary relevance, they will be discussed in more detail.

"Development" and "Existence" of the Bourgeois Relations of Production

From the notion that the new science [historical materialism] must be understood as the "conscious product of historical movement," it does not at all follow that in it knowledge simply coincides with the historiography of its subject matter. This—in the words of contemporary structuralists—"historicist" interpretation, from Lukács's *History and Class Consciousness* to Marcuse's *Reason and Revolution*, could play such a considerable role in the literature on Marxism and history because it points out the moment which was decisive for differentiating the Marxist from the Hegelian dialectic. For Hegel as well as Marx, reality is process: "negative" totality. In Hegelianism, this process appears as a system of reason, that is, as a closed ontology, from which human history sinks to the level of being its derivative, a mere instance of its application. By contrast, Marx emphasizes the independence and openness of historical development, which cannot be reduced to a speculative logic that all being must forever obey. Hence "negativity" comes to refer to something that is fixed in time, while "totality" implies the whole of the modern relations of production. Particularly in the *Grundrisse*, the "rough draft" of *Capital*, Marx derives these relations of production in a concrete-historical manner. They do not, he writes, develop "out of nothing . . . nor from the womb of the self-developing Idea; but from within and in antithesis to the existing development of production and the inherited, traditional relations of property."[11] However, once it has emerged, the bourgeois condition constitutes a system which can be explained in its own terms. The "conditions of its becoming," Marx writes, using Hegelian categories, pass over into "results of its presence."[12] Certainly an immanent presentation of the system has its limits, for when carried out rigorously, it immediately refers back "toward a past lying behind this system."[13] Conversely—and here Marx goes beyond Hegel—the analysis leads "to the points at which the suspension of the present form of production relations gives signs of its becoming—foreshadowings of the future."[14]

Therefore, to the extent to which Marx combats bourgeois economics, which views "capital as an eternal and natural (not historical) form of production,"[15] a shift from the logical to the historical, as well as a reference to the past and future development of the present, is necessary. Of course, we should note the manner in which history comes into play here, as a constructed concept (*konstruierter Begriff*), not as narrative history filled with content. The latter constitutes the indispensable horizon of Marxist research, not in any sense its theme.[16] The critique of political economy—a methodologically essential standpoint—analyses capital and the historical "first stages of its becoming,"[17] viewing the latter as lying beyond capital yet preserved and augmented by capital itself. As a result, for Marx it is unnecessary to "write the actual history of the relations of production" if one wants to develop "the laws of bourgeois economics."[18]

Precisely for this reason, in *Capital* Marx energetically stresses that the process of cognition is characterized by a relative autonomy in face of its object and, hence, does not simply reproduce the historical process of this object:

Reflection on the forms of human life, hence also scientific analysis of those forms, takes a course directly opposite to their real development. Reflection begins *post festum*, and therefore with the results of the process of development already at hand. The forms which stamp products as commodities and which are therefore the preliminary requirements for the circulation of commodities, already possess the fixed quality of natural forms of social life before man seeks to give an account not of their historical character, for in his eyes they are immutable, but of their content and meaning.[19]

The Cognitive Primacy of the Logical over the Historical

The subjective and objective beginnings of knowing are as little identical to one another as are the conceptual mediation and real history of a thing. In this matter Marx follows the critical method of Feuerbach, who had already argued that "only he whose result stands in direct contradiction to his *conscious beginning* is a truly genetic thinker."[20] This expresses only a surface, and hence provisional and "transcendable" truth. Thus Marx's major work [*Capital*] does not (as one might at first expect) begin with the developmental history of capitalist relationships but rather with the immediately given, everyday fact that the wealth of capitalist societies appears as "an immense collection of commodities."[21] From the abstraction of the commodity, the analysis elevates its determinate forms to the level of concrete categories: exchange, money, circulation of commodities, and finally capital. Only subsequently does Marx deal with the actual labor process as such, a process which temporally precedes the circumstances expressed in the categories. In fact, Marx first treats material relevant to the emergence of the capitalist mode of production in the twenty-fourth chapter of volume 1 of *Capital*. There it appears under the title of "primitive accumulation," that is, as the "process which operates two transformations, whereby the social means of subsistence and production are turned into capital, and the immediate producers are turned into wage laborers."[22]

Marx would not have been successful in unfolding the content of the historical presuppositions of capital's emergence had he not first grasped the essence of capital theoretically. He would not even have known where and how they were to be found. It is for this reason, according to commentators such as M. M. Rosenthal, that the chapter on primitive accumulation "only has the purpose of confirming and illustrating with actual history the origin of capital disclosed by logic."[23] As strange as it may sound at first, the mature Marx placed the history of capital on scientific foundations by proceeding on an abstract-theoretical rather than a historiographic level. In adhering strictly to the logic of capital, and thereby disregarding all moments of the empirical course of events which interfere with this logic and are thus nonessential to it, Marx comes closer to the historical content of empirical history than he would have had he been content with chronologically following developments immediately at hand. Whoever studies the materialist dialectic must confront the contradiction that, on the one hand, its founders did not allow themselves to be impressed by the vicissitudes of the real historical process—in Marx's words, they primarily investigated the "ready-made world of capital"[24]—whereas, on the other hand, they tacitly assumed at all levels of their analysis that the "economic structure of capitalist society" emerged historically out of the "economic structure of feudal society."[25] Without abandoning a materialist basis (all conceptual operations in their work rest, directly or indirectly, on the movement of the sensuous, that is, the material world), the theoretical thinking of Marx and Engels assumes a "constructive" (*konstruktiven*) character. It contains history in concentrated form rather than its unmediated copy.[26]

It is particularly important to stress the above in view of the fact that Engels—intent on making the reading public conscious of the qualitatively new element of Marx's method—in his famous review of *The Contribution to the Critique of Political Economy*, had to stress the unity of, rather than the difference between, the logical and the historical within materialism. He wrote that the "German political economy" initiated by Marx has as its "essential foundation ... the materialist conception of history."[27] This conception, in turn, would be unthinkable, Engels continues, without the "exceptional historical sense"[28] of Hegel, the first thinker who attempted "to set forth ... a science in its specific inner coherence,"[29] one bound up with the coherence of the historical process. Engels here accentuates the Hegel-Marx parallelism between the "evolution of ideas" and the "evolution of universal history"[30] more than is justifiable either in terms of textual grounding or in relation to the interest of a theory that wants to avoid vulgar Marxist misunderstandings.

Engels emphasizes how very eager Marx is to ground in a new, namely materialist, way the "abstract, distorted manner" of the process of cognition present in Hegel. Marx does so, Engels writes, by grounding this process "in history."[31] The point was to bring to a scientifically usable form the dialectic which, even in its speculative [Hegelian] version, "had . . . coped with the whole of the former logic and metaphysics with the greatest of ease."[32] As a critical method of political economy, the dialectic can be either logically or historically accentuated. Marx opts for a "logical form of approach"[33] to his material in order not to explode its immanence with theoretically superfluous secondary matters. But, Engels continues, the logical method deviates from historical method only in a relative sense. Each is reflected in the other. The logical (theoretical or, as Marx also said, analytic) method

is . . . indeed nothing but the historical method, only stripped . . . of diverting chance occurrences. The point where this history begins must also be the starting point of the train of thought, and its further progress will be simply the reflection in abstract and theoretically consistent form of the historical course. Though the reflection is corrected, it is corrected in accordance with laws provided by the actual historical course, since each factor can be examined at the stage of development where it reaches its full maturity, its classical form.[34]

In the abstract sense, it is correct that materialist philosophy requires ongoing contact with objective reality—which possesses its own self-movement—and also that its categories do not express timeless essences (ontological structures) but rather "forms of thought which are socially valid, and therefore objective, for the relations of production belonging to this historically determined mode of social production."[35] Even the most abstract

categories—Marx forcefully demonstrates this in connection
with "labor"—are valid only in the context of specific relationships. Engels also never tires of emphasizing that the historical
and the logical, seen as a whole, coincide with and form a unity
which really is grounded in the historical. "Only the historical
gives determinate form to abstraction and predestines its place
and its role in [Marx's] theoretical system."[36] Engels's review also
mentions numerous historical documents, excurses, and inserts
of an illustrative nature in Marx's economic works. They both
interrupt and confirm its logical nature by always referring it
back to real and concrete history.

The founders of Marxism were proven historians (and au-
thorities on the important bourgeois historiography of their
century). They were just as preoccupied with questions concerning economic and social history (questions which were first the-
matized in a rigorous manner through their materialist method)
as they were with the political history of the time, not to mention
their detailed knowledge and insights into historical literature,
above all in the area of economic scholarship. Their works on
the revolutions of 1848, Engels's *The Peasant War in Germany* and
Marx's *The Eighteenth Brumaire of Louis Bonaparte* and *Theories of
Surplus Value*, come to mind. In these writings historical development provides, in Engels's words, "a natural clue, which the
critique could take as a natural point of departure."[37] In them,
sequences of time and of ideas penetrate one another.

On the other hand, the relationship between the logical and
the historical methods presents itself differently when we turn
our attention in a structural manner to the problems concerning
the whole of bourgeois economics. Then logic and history—this
becomes clear in Marx—separate and are connected only in a
highly mediated way. Of course, the unity of method remains
intact: the "historical content" still constitutes the "real foundation"[38] of the thought process (in its specifically contemporary
meaning as historical writing) which is nomothetically oriented.

This latter approach is emancipated from slavishly "reflecting" factual material. When the neo-Kantian, Lange, in his book on the labor question, claimed that Marx moved "with singular freedom" through the empirical material, Marx accepted the notion positively and explained: "He hasn't the least idea that the 'free movement through the material' is nothing but a paraphrase for the method of dealing with this material—that is, the dialectical method."[39] From this follows the, at first glance astonishing, sentence from Marx in the very important *Introduction to the Critique of Political Economy*:

It would therefore be unfeasible and wrong to let the economic categories follow one another in the same sequence as that in which they were historically decisive. Their sequence is determined, rather, by their relation to one another in modern bourgeois society, which is precisely the opposite of that which seems to be their natural order or which corresponds to historical development.[40]

Analytic and Dialectical Reason in Hegel

The primacy of the logical is to be understood in a cognitive sense, and not as if the categories are the existential ground of the reality that is mediated through them. Similarly, it is clear that the Marxist concept of a constructive "mode of presentation" (*Darstellungsweise*) of the scientific object, which is formally distinguished from the (in the broadest sense empirical) "mode of inquiry"[41] (*Forschungsweise*), is taken from the Hegelian system. Unquestionably, in making this distinction, Marx was thinking of Hegel's argument in the introductory reflections of his *Philosophy of Nature* concerning the relationship between (scientific) analysis and (speculative) dialectic:

The material prepared out of experience by physics is taken by the philosophy of nature at the point to which physics has brought it, and reconstituted without any further reference to experience as the basis of verification. Physics must therefore work together with philosophy so that the universalized understanding which it provides may be translated into the Notion by showing how this universal, as an intrinsically necessary whole, proceeds out of the Notion. The philosophic manner of presentation is not arbitrary; it does not stand on its head for a while because it has gotten tired of using its legs . . . the ways of physics are not adequate to the Notion, and for that reason advances have to be made.[42]

What raises the "rational" presentation of a structured whole above the "understanding" activity of inductive research in individual areas is the structure of categories proper to it—in Hegel's words, the "range of universal thought determinations . . . as it were the diamond-net into which we bring everything in order to make it intelligible."[43] Thinking which pushes forward to abstract generalities and rests satisfied with them is indispensable, but it is unable to penetrate the determinate content. It remains, according to Hegel, "split-up, dismembered, particularized, separated, and lacking in any necessary connection within itself."[44] Hence analytic knowing, contrary to its own claim, remains an "abstract" and therefore limited empiricism. For Hegel, placing the mere working up of sensuous data above reflection on them constitutes a "wrong way." Further, "Intuition has to be submitted to thought, so that what has been dismembered may be restored to simple universality through thought. This contemplated unity is the Notion, which contains the determinate differences simply as an immanent and self-moving unity."[45]

The Marxian Ascent from the Abstract to the Concrete

Marx takes up—on a materialist basis—the Hegelian method of ascending from the abstract to the concrete and, therefore, Hegel's critique of conceptless empiricism. For Marx as well as Hegel, scientific knowledge has a "presenting" (*darstellenden*) rather than a descriptive character. The "concrete" at which it aims is precisely the opposite of what common sense means by the term (the classifiable individual fact) but refers instead to a synthetic knowledge, a conceptualized "unity of the diverse."[46] The Marxist dialectic resists (as did the Hegelian) the strict dichotomy between facts and ideas. It is not a "subsumption of a mass of 'cases' under a general principle."[47] Rather it theorizes that universal social production should be grasped as a concrete-universal. Particular constituent elements such as distribution, exchange, and consumption are not a chaotic sum of fixed data organized in a manner external to them. Rather, according to Marx, they constitute objective "members of a totality ... distinctions within a unity,"[48] which is established by the overarching moment of production.

In line with this argument, Marx explicitly rejects the merely "analytical method" of classical economics, which is not interested in "how the various forms came into being" but believes instead that it can immediately and completely reduce these forms to their unity. Marx argues that it holds this position because it dogmatically "starts out from them [the forms] as given premises."[49] Marx leaves no doubt that analytic thinking is a necessary foundation of "genetic presentation, of comprehending of the real, formative process in its different phases."[50] But because this process—the real object of knowledge—does not coincide immediately with the real course of history, analysis at most can (as demonstrated by the beginnings of economic scholarship in the seventeenth century) "discover . . . a small number of determinant, abstract general relations such as labor, division of labor, money, value, etc."[51] Presented in this manner, they remain isolated moments of a totality whose living structure is not actually derived from the necessity of its own concept.

However, to the degree to which these categories, which emerged from history and were developed through analysis, "had been . . . established and abstracted"[52] and had lost the trace of their empirical origins, the economists adopted another method. Now their systems began to ascend from the simple to the complex, and they turned from labor and its division, from needs and exchange value, to the state, commerce between states (politics), and the world market.[53] For Marx, this shift constitutes the "scientifically correct method."[54] This method is not at all (as even Marcuse said, in a manner that in light of the contemporary state of the discussion is at least subject to misunderstanding) primarily a "historical method."[55] However, it does contain, in the form of a conceptual concentrate, the history of political economy as science (and as empirical reality). The Marxian method is a logical process, which takes as its point of departure a "chaotic conception of the whole" and, by means of more abstract steps, arrives at a "rich totality of many determinations and relations."[56] The method's dialectical structure expresses itself in the equal consideration it gives to the moments of the "false" and the "true," that is, to the historically surpassed route of early economics, along which "the full conception was evaporated to yield an abstract determination," as well as the deductive path of later economics, on which "the abstract determinations lead toward a reproduction of the concrete."[57]

In this connection, Marx also explains his relation to Hegel. The view that logical operations, in contrast to a sensuous inventory of facts, make possible knowledge that is more concrete and richer in content approaches Hegel's

illusion of conceiving the real as the product of thought concentrating itself, probing its own depths, and unfolding itself out of itself, by itself, whereas the method of rising from the abstract to the concrete is the only way in which thought appropriates the concrete, reproduces it [as something permeated with concepts] as the concrete in the mind. But this is by no means the process by which the concrete itself comes into being.[58]

Of course, this nonidentity of knowledge with the real genesis of the known not only indicates the fundamental materialist circumstance that the "concrete totality [as] a totality of thoughts" is always the product of "the working up of observation and representation into concepts."[59] These concepts do reveal the essence but do not (as moments of "the" concept) create it. The nonidentity of knowledge and its object points to something more specific, namely, that the Marxian method, regardless of its difference from the Hegelian method, accepts the latter's highly complex critique of empiricism so far as it—as has been repeatedly emphasized here—accords to the actual theoretical process far greater autonomy than is evident in most interpretations.

"Inquiry" (Forschung) and "Presentation" (Darstellung) in the Speculative Dialectic

Marx's suggestions, in the afterword to the second edition of *Capital*, concerning the unity of and distinction between "inquiry" and "presentation," suggestions that were rigorously carried out in his material studies, had their exact model in Hegel, whose great reflections on the relation between empiricism (in the individual disciplines) and concrete history, on the one hand, and philosophical theory, on the other, are strewn throughout his whole work. I will now discuss a passage, unfortunately rather extensive, from Hegel's *Lectures on the History of Philosophy*, a passage that refers to Francis Bacon. In spite of its speculative language, it anticipates Marx's project of a "dialectical presentation" especially clearly:

Empiricism is not merely an observing, hearing, feeling, etc., a perception of the individual: for it really sets to work . . . to discover laws. Now because it does this, it comes within the territory of the Notion—it . . . thus prepares the empirical material for the Notion, so that the latter can revise it . . . for its use. If the science is perfected, the Idea must certainly issue forth from itself; science as such no longer commences from the empirical. But in order that this science may come into existence, we must have the progression from the individual and particular to the universal—an activity which is a reaction to the given material of empiricism in order to bring about its reconstruction. . . . Without the working out of the empirical sciences on their own account, Philosophy could not have reached further than it did with the ancients. The whole of the Idea in itself is science as perfected and complete; but on the other side is the beginning, the process of its origination. This process of the origination of science is different from its process in itself when it is complete, just as is the process of the history of Philosophy and that of Philosophy itself. Every science begins with principles. In the beginning these are the results of the particular, but if the science is completed, they are made the starting point. The case is similar with Philosophy; the working out of the empirical side has really become the essential condition of the Idea, so that it can reach its full development. . . . In consciousness, it then adopts the attitude of having cut away the bridge from behind it; it appears to be free only in its ether to launch forth, and to develop without resistance in this medium; but it is another matter, to attain this ether as well as development within it."[60]

Let us reflect on these ideas of Hegel's that were of such importance to Marx's conception of science. First, it is apparent that the great idealist, Hegel, does not at all haughtily brush aside Bacon's principle of methodically knowing individual facts but rather considers it as necessary, especially for the speculative philosophy itself. In his view, the finite is as constitutive for the infinite as the latter is for the former. No absolute contradiction exists between sensuous and conceptual knowledge, all experience contains "theoretical" elements, and thus a pure immediacy is impossible. Hegel accepts the sciences that had developed since the Renaissance, for "knowledge from the absolute," if it is not to assert empty theses, requires the extensively and intensively developed "particularity of the content."[61] The latter is provided by concrete inquiries. They provide intellectual labor with the indispensable factual foundation. However, to the extent to which "empiricism" does not exhaust itself in a mere piling up of the sensuous given but rather aims at grasping objective laws, it already finds itself, as Hegel writes, "within the territory of the Notion[62] and prepares the material for it. Consequently there is in Hegel (and in Marx as well) no unbridgeable gap between modern analytic and dialectical science.

The second point which emerges from these considerations is perhaps even more important from a Marxist perspective. Hegel stresses that science (as he understands it: as the "concrete" idea, the "system"), once "complete," must no longer start out from the empirical but from itself. In order to achieve this autonomy, it must, in Hegel's view, rely on "the development of the experiential sciences themselves." In relation to philosophy, however, the task of the latter consists only in becoming dispensable. The speculative science is completed when the "whole of the Idea in itself"[63] is attained with empirical assistance. It floats free, as it were, of its real basis, and the "process of its origination" is reduced to the external, merely abstract "beginning." Although just this loss and reduction demonstrates the dubiousness of idealism, it does not follow that Hegel's thought should be simply rejected. Insofar as the Marxian critique of political economy refers strictly to the bourgeois relations of production, it draws on the Hegelian insight that the "process of origination" of a science must be distinguished from its "process in itself," just as the "process of the history of philosophy [is distinguished from] that of philosophy itself."[64] According to Hegel, in its beginning, every science orients itself to axioms which are the "results of the particular."[65] Once developed, these axioms are governed by their own logical character. Still, Hegel hints that this sphere of "pure" conceptual immanence, removed from all historical development, always contains an illusory (Marx would have said "ideological") moment. The system that is alienated from history nevertheless remains imprisoned in it.

From "System" to History

We now turn to Marx himself. His theory follows Hegel's insofar as he also seeks to present bourgeois society, irrespective of its historical origin, as a closed system, that is, *one explicable in terms of itself*. Marx argues that although this system is the direct result of the conscious acts of living individuals, it blindly and violently establishes itself over against its creators. Because, in economic terms, the value-character of the products of labor first manifests itself on the market in magnitudes of value, which exchange "independently of the will, foreknowledge and action of the exchangers," these magnitudes assume "the form of a movement made by things, and these things, far from being under their control, in fact control them."[66] Hence the often-misunderstood focus of Marx's theory essentially on the object should be understood as a critical theory rather than as a kind of world view or confessional creed. Its goal is that the hitherto unconsciously governing forces should, in the future, be subjected to the consciousness of solidary individuals.[67]

Marx's *Capital* and the studies preliminary to it deal with a condition in which a human creation appears with the merciless harshness of a being in itself. For example, Marx writes that in the money fetish, "a social relation, a definite relation between individuals . . . appears as a metal, as a stone, as a purely physical external thing which can be found, as such, in nature, and which is indistinguishable in form from its natural existence."[68] Theory makes this immediacy transparent only with great difficulty. (In everyday life it remains completely opaque.) The rigidified, thinglike, congealed relationships between people, who are reduced to becoming mere bearers and silent instruments for carrying out these relationships, form a negative totality, which, in turn, is the specific object of dialectical materialism. As has already been emphasized, Marx does not investigate the capitalist world primarily as an economic and social historian but rather does so from the viewpoint of its developed structure, that is, an "existence of value" which has achieved "purity and universality." He abstracts from the history of landed property in which modern capital originated. The latter is a mode of production in which, as Marx writes, "the individual product has ceased to exist for the producer in general . . . and where nothing exists unless it is realized through circulation."[69] For Marx, all historical presuppositions (presuppositions which he had thoroughly studied) of fully developed capital are only those of "its becoming, which," along the lines of Hegel's *Logic*, "are overcome and preserved in its being." They "belong to the history of its formation, but in no way to its *contemporary* history, i.e., not to the real system of the mode of production ruled by it."[70] Marx is dealing with a "system" in the strict deductive sense rather than with a historiographical task, because the form of capital which the system develops produces its own conditions of existence and no longer does so "as conditions of its arising, but as results of its presence."[71] The forms which temporally preceded it lie behind the system just as "the processes by means of which the earth made the transition from a liquid sea of fire and vapor to its present form now lie beyond its life as finished earth."[72]

At first glance, this separation, absent in Marx's early writings, of empirical history and immanent "presentation" of the categories[73] offends against the principle that is continuously and justly stressed in materialist literature: the mutual interpenetration of the historical and the logical. Actually, however, such is not the case. Marx, as I emphasized at the outset, as strange as it may sound at first, comes closer to the real course of history when he proceeds on a logical-constructive path than when he is satisfied with depicting it in its immediate and therefore false concreteness. The method tested in *Capital* (like the Hegelian method) was not a tool external to the subject but rather reproduced its necessary "process in-itself." Its goal is to treat the capitalist process as a whole so that its objective logic, free from accidental as well as ideological accessories, will become evident. Marx himself characterizes the task he had set himself in the following manner: "The work in question is a critique of economic categories or the system of bourgeois economy critically presented. It is a presentation of the system and simultaneously, through the presentation, a criticism."[74] This important double aspect of the Marxist method leads us from the logical back to the historical-theoretical problematic.

We started out from the idea that Marx analyzes the structure of capital by consciously disregarding the particularities of its historical emergence. He focuses on its developed form. Of course, capital appears in its unmediated form as money, for which labor-power is bought as a commodity on the market. Marx investigates the exchange process between commodities and money and then demonstrates the manner in which the latter changes into capital. According to Marx, money originates in circulation and is the "first concept of capital . . . [the] first form in which it appears."[75] As Rosenthal's study underscores, this purely logical analysis simultaneously constitutes the "key to the history of capital,"[76] a history which Marx neglected primarily on systematic grounds. Indirectly, however, Marx showed that bourgeois modes of production necessarily presuppose what he substantively pointed out in the chapter on "primitive accumulation" in *Capital*: that "on the one hand owners of money" and "on the other hand free laborers, sellers of their own labor power,"[77] stand opposite one another. In addition, as Rosenthal also indicates, the Marxian analysis implies that history reproduces itself with every new act of the reproduction of capital. To this extent, "the logical analysis," Rosenthal writes, is "at the same time the historical analysis. The latter only appears as the opposite of the former."[78] In other words, the logical and the historical coincide, although in a very mediated fashion.

How money changes into capital is, first of all, a historical question. Marx recalls that modern society came into being in the sixteenth century with world trade and the world market. The personal relations of domination and bondage resting on landed property were dissolved through the anonymous power of capital, which first appeared as money (property) and as merchant and usury capital: "M-C-C-M . . . ; this movement of buying in order to sell, which makes up the formal aspect of commerce, of capital as merchant capital . . . is the first movement in which exchange value as such forms the content—is not only the form but also its own content." [79] Marx's term, the "determination of the form" (*Formbestimmung*) of trade (an expression that aptly characterizes his scientific interest), theoretically guarantees that, in his words,

we do not need to look back at the history of capital's origins in order to recognize that money is its first form of appearance. Every day the same story is played out before our eyes. Even up to the present day, all new capital, in the first instance, steps onto the stage—i.e. the market, whether it is the commodity-market, the labor-market, or the money-market—in the shape of money, money which has to be transformed into capital by definite processes. [80]

Accordingly the general theory of this transition is not to be developed historically but rather, Marx argues, on the basis of laws which are immanent to commodity exchange.

The parallelism of such formulations to those in Hegel's work is obvious. Just as the idealist system of philosophy, once rounded off and self-defined, left its historical premises behind, like a shedded skin, so the bourgeois relations of production appearing in the money form of capital constitute a system "in process" (*prozessierendes System*) whose functioning must be explained through rigorous conceptual labor.

The Problem of the Starting Point of Science

As is well known, Marx seeks to accomplish a difficult task such as this one by taking as his point of departure the commodity- or value-form of the products of labor. He calls it the "economic cell-form"[81] of bourgeois society, one which makes it possible to reveal it as an "intensive" totality. Like a Leibnitzian monad, the commodity reflects in itself the whole world conditioned by its structure, a point to which Lenin drew particular attention. In his summary of Hegel's *Science of Logic*, he investigates Hegel's theory of the Notion, especially from an epistemological view-point, and thus establishes that the

formation of [abstract] concepts [already includes] conscious-ness of the law-governed character of the objective connection of the world. . . . Just as the simple value-form, the individual act of exchange of one given commodity for another, already includes in undeveloped form all the main contradictions of capitalism—so the simplest generalization . . . already denotes man's ever-deeper cognition of the objective connection of the world.[82]

And elsewhere, again alluding to the theoretical process in *Capital*, he writes, "The beginning—the most simple, ordinary, mass, immediate 'Being': the single commodity [*Sein* in political economy]. The analysis of it as a social relation. The *double* analysis, deductive and inductive—logical and historical [forms of value]."[83] In other words, Lenin, continues, Marx's *Capital* also offers a "history of capitalism," but, as he expressly adds, it does so in the form of an "analysis of the *concepts* forming it up."[84]

Here Lenin was thinking of the systematic construction of the first volume of *Capital*, a construction which is simultaneously a historical and a logical one insofar as the sequence commodity-money-capital, with which Marxist economics begins, reflects the real process which was supposed to have led to the origin of capital. Since the prehistory of this process is characterized by the production and circulation of commodities, the logical beginning of Marxian analysis coincides with the genetic beginning of the object it studies. As Engels puts it, the line of reasoning must certainly begin at the point where actual history begins.[85] But it would unquestionably be wrong to claim on this account that Marx wanted to describe the development of modern society because *Capital* begins with the analysis of the commodity. As we know, the reason is a specifically theoretical one. The commodity appears as the "elementary form"[86] of bourgeois wealth, and "the commodity-form is the most general and the most undeveloped form of bourgeois production."[87] It is—and this is what matters—the abstract, in the Hegelian sense, something conceptually still unspecified and poor in content, from which an ascent is made with an inner necessity to more concrete, more differentiated knowledge by way of highly subtle abstractions. As a result, there exists a developmental-logical connection between the categories produced by the analysis of commodities, the insight into the objective antagonisms of the bourgeois world, and the prediction of its collapse. What the beginning implies, the end confirms. For, as Hegel writes, the "progress from that which forms the beginning is to be regarded as only a further determination of it; hence that which forms the starting point of the development remains at the base of all that follows and does not vanish from it." Although it gradually becomes increasingly mediated, the beginning is "the foundation which is present and preserved throughout the entire subsequent development, remaining completely immanent in its further determinations."[88]

The "Progressive-Regressive" Method

Hence the—at first curious—situation must be considered that the subjective advance of knowledge is objectively, in regard to

its content, a step backward. Here Marx followed the structure
of Hegel's *Science of Logic* (and, as Lefebvre and Sartre put it, its
"progressive-regressive" method). In *The Science of Logic*, Hegel
discusses the recent view that philosophy, first of all, must be a
"quest" because it can begin only with "hypothetical and problematic truths."[89] He was impressed with the related and clearly
developing interest in the speculative problematic of the "beginning" and used the opportunity mainly to come to an understanding of the "meaning of logical advance," above all, of the
view claiming "that progress in philosophy is rather a retrogres-
sion and a grounding . . . by means of which we first obtain the
result that what we began with is not something merely arbitrarily assumed but is in fact, in part the truth, in part the primary
truth."[90] Hegel elaborates on and specifies this view—a view important for Marxist theory—in saying

that the advance is a retreat into the ground, to what is primary
and true, on which depends, and in fact, from which originates,
that with which the beginning is made. . . . This last, the ground
is then also that form which the first proceeds, that which at first
appeared as an immediacy. . . . The essential requirement for
the science of logic is not . . . that the beginning be a pure immediacy, but rather that the whole of the science be within itself
a circle in which the first is also the last and the last is also the
first.[91]

We will now investigate the modifications undergone by this
important Hegelian theorem as it reappeared in Marxian
economics.

In Marx's view, the beginning and end of the analysis of bourgeois processes of production are determined by "the real and
the concrete."[92] In his important outline of a materialist method,
Introduction to a Critique of Political Economy (written in 1857–1858),
Marx understands the "real and concrete" to be the foundation
of all "perspectives and conceptions," which he intends to analyze conceptually. It emerges twice—as the "point of departure"
of the process of cognition and as its "result."[93] In the first case,

it refers to the closed immediacy of the wealth of commodities typical of capitalist society (whose structure, which is decisive for the whole epoch, Marx illuminates through "microscopic"[94] analysis of individual aspects). In the latter case, the "real and concrete" refers to the intellectually mastered whole of such unmediated facts, that is, their inner, lawlike coherence, at which science aims. But this coherence, no less than the logical operations which mediate it, may not be "mystified."[95] Marx criticizes Hegelian philosophy for such mystification. Since "conceptual thinking" is not the "real human being" and "the conceptual world as such is [not] the only reality,"[96] the first immediacy, what in conventional terms is called the "concrete," coincides with the concrete of a higher order, which it proves itself to be once it has been theoretically penetrated. Whether theory succeeds in penetrating the concrete, the real object "retains its autonomous existence outside the head just as before; namely as long as the head's conduct is merely speculative, merely theoretical."[97]

The materialist dialectic of the actual process of cognition develops between "point of departure" and "result"; both, considered separately, are abstract moments. In view of the historical-theoretical dimension of this dialectic, we will examine it once again. Hegel, in his *Science of Logic*, considers the progressive development of the idea (it is closer to the development from "being" to "essence," becoming totally transparent as the notion) from "a state of knowledge that is undeveloped and devoid of content [to] one full of content and truly grounded."[98] He views this as a stage-by-stage return of the empty beginning into its "ground," which first gives it full content. This is an idea which the mature Marx also takes up. He also carefully investigates the progression from external, surface "appearances" of economic reality to their "essence" (inner laws); that is, he also returns to the "ground" of the "existence" of these "appearances." Marx, as well as Hegel, is convinced that "retrogressive grounding of the beginning . . . and the progressive further determining of it"[99] takes place *uno actu*. Certainly—this makes all the difference—Hegel's logical categories, when translated into political-economic ones, assume a completely different character. Above all, they lose their timeless closed validity because the "ground," which mediates the beginning—the given commodity-world—and toward which knowledge moves, is not an absolute concept but rather the history which bursts all logical immanence and can never be spiritualized.

However much Marx, in deriving the concept of capital from the economic form of exchange (and not from its natural or historical content), endeavors to explain the mechanism of bourgeois production completely within its own terms, he is not ready to capitulate in the face of the existing system as such. Indeed he writes that it is superfluous "to write the real history of the relations of production" in order to "develop the laws of bourgeois economy."[100] But, he continues, it is precisely the logical method, apparently removed from anything historical, which "indicates the points at which historical investigation must enter in, or where bourgeois political economy points beyond itself to earlier historical modes of production,[101] [to a] past lying behind this system."[102] This past is depicted by Marx in chapter 24 of the first volume of *Capital*, dealing with "primitive accumulation"—the real development of the essence: the (Hegelian) "ground" of that with which the theoretical labor of that work begins.

The Location of Capitalism in Universal History

Bourgeois society is methodologically so important for dialectical materialism because it is "the most developed and the most complex historic organization of production."[103] Marx stresses the degree to which the appropriate understanding of the past depends on the "correct grasp of the present."[104] The critical analysis of the given structure, according to Marx, "allows insights into the structure and the relations of production of all the vanished social formations out of whose ruins and elements it built itself up."[105] The richly articulated system is the basis on which the history which determines it can be revealed, not the reverse. This insight distinguishes the dialectic from shallow evolutionism. In both natural and social history, "the intimations of higher development" among lower levels can be understood only "after the higher development is already known."[106] Hence the specifically bourgeois political economy provides the "key" to the social life forms that preceded it. For Marx, this merely underscored the necessity of not forgetting the difference while grasping the identity between bourgeois political economy and its predecessors. Bourgeois categories (and the circumstances that find expression through them) may also, Marx writes, emerge before the bourgeois era: "developed, or stunted, or caricatured," always, however, "with an essential difference."[107] Marx then adds a remarkable reflection on the concept of historical development:

The so-called historical presentation of development is founded, as a rule, on the fact that the latest form regards the previous ones as steps leading up to itself, and since it is only rarely and only under quite specific conditions able to criticize itself [in a fundamental sense] it always conceives them one-sidedly. The Christian religion was able to be of assistance in reaching an objective understanding of earlier mythologies only when its own self-criticism had been accomplished to a certain degree, so to speak, potentially. Likewise, bourgeois economics arrived at an understanding of feudal, ancient, oriental economics only after the self-criticism of bourgeois society had begun.[108]

From the standpoint of universal history, capitalism marks a sort of high point. Once present as a functioning system, it serves theoretically as a principle of explanation of its past as well as future development and hence also explains precisely those driving forces which undermine its systematic character.

When Marx discusses the manner in which money is transformed into capital, he feels compelled to add that "the dialectical form of presentation is correct only if it recognizes its own limits,"[109] these being the points at which living history penetrates into a nature-like, rigidified system. The general concept of capital can be derived in a purely deductive manner from "simple circulation" because in the bourgeois mode of production, the latter "itself exists only as a presupposition of capital and as something which in turn presupposes it." But this does not (as Marx remarks with an evident sarcasm directed at Hegel) transform capital "into the incarnation of an eternal idea."[110] Rather it shows "how in reality capital must first enter as a *necessary* form only in production based on exchange value."[111] Considerable difficulties emerge, of course, concerning the lawfulness of this transition from circulation into capital, when Marx presents its historical character in a logical, rather than historiographical, manner. He writes, "The simple circulation is . . . an abstract sphere of the bourgeois production process as a whole, which . . . through its own determinations proves itself to be . . . a mere phenomenal form (*Erscheinungsform*) of the process of industrial capital which lies behind it, results from its and produces it."[112] Money becomes capital by being exchanged for noncapital, that is, for the labor capacities of individuals.

Marxian economics is a system and at the same time not a system, for what forms the totality of bourgeois society is equally that which ceaselessly pushes beyond it. As an immanent critic, Marx assumes that the relationships he investigates exist "in pure form corresponding to their concept."[113] But as a critic, he knows how little (not only in England in that period) that is the case. Socialism cannot rest content with philistine research contributions; rather it sees itself as the "antithesis to political economy," which, of course, as Marx always acknowledges, finds its point of departure "in the works of classical political economy itself, especially in Ricardo, who must be regarded as its complete and final expression."[114] Marx views Ricardo so favorably because he is essentially different from the superficial, vulgar empiricist economists in that he bluntly articulates the antagonistic character of the dominant relations of production. Further, in his studies of liberal competition, Marx demonstrates that Ricardo is sharp enough at least to raise the question of the transient nature of the capitalist condition, one which he personally viewed as an incontestable natural form of human life.

Competition—this is its negative, historically effective side—dissolves the collective constraints and restrictions which are naturally bound to prebourgeois stages. Marx immediately observes, in a manner indebted to the critique of ideology, that in the analysis of this process it is important to avoid the persistent error which suggests that the "absolute mode of existence of free individuality"[115] arises out of it. What, from the perspective of many-sided, developed competition, appears as a limit of earlier modes of production, was in these modes themselves the "inherent limits . . . within which they spontaneously developed and moved,"[116] that is, not an actual deficiency at all. Marx stresses that

these limits became barriers only after the forces of production and the relations of intercourse had developed sufficiently to enable capital as such to emerge as the dominant principle of production. The limits which it tore down were barriers to its motion, its development and realization. It is by no means the case [in contrast to what bourgeois apologetics still claim today] that it thereby suspended all limits, or all barriers, but rather only the limits not corresponding to it, which were barriers to it. Within its own limits . . . it feels itself free and free of barriers, i.e., as limited only by itself, only by its own conditions of life.[117]

The aspect of free competition referring to the completed "system" of bourgeois society is even more important for Marx. In it capital relates "to itself as another capital."[118] Its "inner laws," which appear in the "preliminary historic stages of its development" merely as anticipatory "tendencies," from now on are "posited as laws" and actually become effective as such. Marx continues, "Production founded on capital for the first time posits itself in the forms adequate to it only insofar as and to the extent that free competition develops, for it is the free development . . . of its conditions and of itself as the process that continuously reproduces these conditions."[119] Marx objects to interpreting the role of competition in an overly optimistic manner. In his view, it is not living individuals (and their needs) who are emancipated by competition but rather capital, which, with free competition, begins its "real development."[120] What is inherent in the general nature and concept of competition now presents itself as the "external necessity"[121] which dominates the many individual capitals. Their competition (which includes the competition of the worker with his or her equals) means, quite simply, that they "force the inherent determinants" of capital in general "upon one another and upon themselves."[122]

As long as the bourgeois mode of production is the most appropriate historical form for advancing the universal growth of the productive forces that serve the human species, the ideology that goes along with this mode of production contains a moment of truth. According to this ideology, of necessity "the movement of individuals within the pure conditions of capital *appears* as their freedom; which is then also again dogmatically propounded as such through constant reflection back on the barriers torn down by free competition."[123] To the extent to which the "reciprocal compulsion" which competing capitals "exercise upon one another" leads to the "*free* [and] at the same time the *real* development of wealth as capital," competition becomes a scientifically and economically decisive category. Even Ricardo presupposes its "absolute predominance in order to be able to study and to formulate the adequate laws of capital."[124] The higher the level of competition, the more successful this effort will be. It is the former which, as the argument goes, determines how purely the forms of movement of capital manifest themselves.

Marx then shows that Ricardo, by firmly adhering to these premises, was compelled to make an admission which transcended the bourgeois horizon. Objectively, what appeared in his conceptualization is "the *historic nature* of capital and the limited character of free competition, which is just the free movement of capitals and nothing else, i.e., their movement within conditions which belong to no previous, dissolved stages, but are its own conditions." [125] That free competition of this kind moves into the center, not least of all in the political struggles of the preceding century, does not mean that the capital-relation is grounded in the movements of many capitals. Rather, the predominance of competition implies that capital as a historic life form has in fact already established itself and only appears in the facts in the forground of the circulation sphere. This was stated, albeit without consequences, by the best representatives of classical economics. In particular, it did not enable them to see that the ahistorical "systematic nature" (*Systematizität*) of the existing society is itself historically produced. Ultimately the classical economists fall into what Marx, in the section of *Capital* on the fetish character of commodities, calls objectified illusion (*gegendständlichen Schein*). This illusion is reinforced, Marx writes, by the movement of capital, "according to its own laws" as soon as it no longer needs the "crutches of past modes of production or of those which will pass with its rise." [126] Certainly this systematic nature of the bourgeois world proves itself to be ever more fragile. This is so because in capital (whose historical victory it once made possible) the expansion of the productive forces, and therefore human freedom, come up against a barrier which cannot be transcended in a manner immanent to the system but rather only through a qualitative leap beyond it. Marx's theory points to the familiar conclusion that capital assumes forms which appear to complete its domination—increasing the concentration of capital gradually dismantles free competition—while in truth it announces its collapse.

Marx argues that when liberalism, in its classical form and in its contemporary extension, equates the "negation of free competition" in the planned economy with the "negation of individual freedom," it overlooks the fact that its kind of "individual freedom is . . . at the same time . . . the complete subjugation of individuality under social conditions [which] assume the form of objective powers, even of overpowering objects" [127] and which have made themselves independent of individuals. For Marx, the recognition of these objects as historical products of human beings, and the condemnation of their separation of the latter from the objectified instruments of their labor as a reprehensible form of domination, constitutes "an enormous awareness" [128] which the theory (itself growing out of these relations) must articulate or even construct for the first time. The characteristic specific to the method of the mature Marx (this much is evident from what has been discussed up to this point) is that it serves the explosive power of the historical dialectic by following the path of logic. History which transcends the present does not enter his system as an externally introduced product of his world view but rather (at least according to his ideas) is derived strictly from its own premises. References to the past lying behind the bourgeois world appear, polemically, everywhere in *Capital*. They do so without (before the well-known twenty-fourth chapter) either becoming directly constitutive for the cognition process or finding their location in the "logic of presentation."

In order to transform money into capital, its owner must find the free worker (the modern proletarian) on the market. The question as to why he comes across this worker in the sphere of circulation does not interest him at all. In the labor market, he quite rightly sees a "particular branch of the commodity-market."[129] And to begin with, the question interests Marx just as little. As he writes, "We confine ourselves to the fact theoretically, as he does practically."[130] In other words, Marx enters into the systematic presuppositions of his object, but he does not capitulate before them:

One thing . . . is clear: nature does not produce on the one hand owners of money or commodities, and on the other hand men possessing nothing but their own labor-power. This relation has no basis in *natural history*, nor does it have a social basis common to all periods of human history. It is clearly the result of a past historical development, the product of many economic revolutions, of the extinction of a whole series of older formations of social production.

The economic categories already discussed similarly bear a historical imprint. Definite historical conditions are involved in the existence of the produce as a commodity. . . . The *various forms of money* . . . indicate very different levels of the process of social production. Yet we know . . . that a relatively feeble development of commodity circulation suffices for the creation of these forms. It is otherwise with *capital*. The *historical* conditions of its existence are by no means given with the mere circulation of money and commodities. It arises only when the owner of the means of production and subsistence finds the *free* worker available, on the market, as the seller of his own labor-power. And *this one historical precondition* comprises a world's history. Capital, therefore, announces from the outset a new epoch in the process of social production.[131]

This passage underscores Marx's view that it is no longer necessary to uncover the developmental-historical origin of capital once it has developed and the moments of its formation have "disappeared" into a system which allows for a rigorous, immanent critique. This principle, which is absolutely essential for dialectical thinking, nevertheless requires a correction because it illuminates only one side of Marx's relationship to the classical economists. When one bears in mind that from the outset he studied Smith and Ricardo with reference to their own results and intentions, it becomes clear that his critique pursued a qualitatively different goal than they themselves did. It is not out of mere archival interest that he returns again and again to the nodal points at which the immanent presentation must give way to a historical one. Rather the reason is found in the analysis itself. The analysis which defines the bourgeois system in relation to its past indicates just as much that this system was relative to a "movement of becoming," which it transcends: "Just as, on one side the prebourgeois phases appear as *merely histori-cal*, i.e., suspended presuppositions, so do the contemporary conditions of production likewise appear as engaged in *suspending themselves* and hence in positing the historic presuppositions for a new state of society." [132]

Again it becomes apparent—at a point decisive for Marx's whole conceptual framework—that the logical method, properly understood, is also the most appropriate method for understanding historical development. It permits the grasp of the antagonistic whole, in Engels's words, "at the stage of development where it reaches its . . . classical form." [133] As Hegel writes in *The Science of Logic*, "The highest maturity, the highest stage, which anything can attain is that in which its downfall begins." [134] It is on the basis of just this view, one which permeates all of his individual assertions, that Marx observes capitalist reality. [135] He knows how far its immediate forms of appearance fall short of what his theory offers in insights into its essence. However much the false society—for an indeterminate time—may grow, it is a self-dissolving form of the world spirit, one condemned by the court of universal history.

Against the background of these considerations, we can now look at the complex relation of system and process, logic and history in the mature Marx, and can do so in its more fundamental aspect.

Valid and Invalid Aspects of the Structuralist Marx Interpretation

In *Capital* Marx advocates anything but an unreflected historicism, in which knowledge runs directly parallel to the chronological course of events. Structuralist interpreters, such as Althusser and Poulantzas, are correct up to this point. Beyond this point, when they flatly deny the constitutive role of Hegelian logic for Marx's economic work and announce a "theoretical antihumanism [and] antihistoricism,"[136] agreement comes to an end, for Marx's texts offer no evidence to support such an interpretation. In *Capital* Marx does not, as the structuralists have claimed, reject either the theme of history or that of human nature as being ideological as such. On the contrary, in the later Marx (as is evident not least of all in the *Grundrisse* of 1857) we are dealing with a second appropriation of Hegel, especially the Hegel of *The Science of Logic*. This work is as important for Marx's political-economic analysis in the 1850s and 1860s as the category of labor taken from the *Phenomenology of the Mind* was for his "self-understanding" (*Selbstverständigung*) in the 1840s. Of course in *Capital* (in this regard one can agree with the structuralists) there is no dogmatically established anthropology, no abstract-humanistic "image of man" external to the scientific process of cognition. But it would be a mistake, on this account, to claim that Marx was a "theoretical antihumanist." His effort to analyze the commodity was implicitly humanistic insofar as it rose above the conventional level of national economy. Because Marx refuses merely to register the reified, pseudo-objective structures of capitalist everyday life but seeks instead to bring the history congealed in them back to life, he comes up against the specifically human, if deformed, reality. Hence, in his view, even capital is not a thing "but a social relation between persons which is mediated through things."[137] The reduction of these people to mere "representatives of the world of commodities"[138] is a negative condition that is yet to be historically transcended, not a scientific norm.

In spite of his undeniable rational interest in history (something which linked him to Kant), Marx in *Capital* does not really proceed historically but rather, schooled in Hegel's *Science of Logic*, aims at the "basis and possibility of a synthetic science, of a system and of a systematic cognition."[139] Like Hegel, Marx finds this kind of knowledge in the methodological progression from the abstract to the concrete, from the universal to the particular. Both of these dialectical thinkers resisted the current sensualism which yielded to the isolated facts given to naive consciousness by viewing them as synonymous with "the concrete" in general. Just because the sensuous appropriation of the world comes more easily to individuals than a strictly conceptual appropriation does, it does not follow that the beginning of the former is "more natural than that which begins from the subject matter in its abstraction and from that proceeds in the opposite direction to its particularization and concrete individualization."[140] Even to pose the question concerning the "more natural" path of cognition is wrong from the outset. In scientific thinking, "a method appropriate to cognition is demanded,"[141] which, for the sake of exactitude, allows the external genesis of the object to be set aside for the time being.

We will now consider the consequences that result from the special way in which Hegel's "method appropriate to cognition" enters into Marx's *Capital*. In so doing we must once again turn to Marx's refracted relationship to material history or, more precisely, to the contradiction that his dialectic simultaneously proceeds historically and unhistorically. It proceeds historically insofar as it views cognition and real events as moments of a developing whole. That is, as Lukács emphasized, it points out, on the one hand, that "all the categories in which human existence is constructed must appear as the determinants of that existence itself (and not merely of the description of that existence)," while on the other hand, "their succession, their coherence and their connection must appear as aspects of the historical process itself."[142] By contrast, the Marxist dialectic proceeds unhistorically, or constructively, as Althusser would put it, by starting out from an existing whole which possesses a complex structure, always pregiven, which, in turn, enables this dialectic to determine the value of the position assigned to all "simple" categories (in relation to "structural," not "linear," causality).[143]

Althusser rightly stresses that Marx guards against the myth of a pure beginning of pure simplicity advocated by a "first philosophy." But the radical dehistoricization of Marxist materialism which Althusser proposes, and which he accomplishes only through an arbitrary use of citations, by no means follows. Certainly Marx views production (to mention a common concept) as always historically determinate "production by social individuals,"[144] who consequently, as Althusser adds, "live in a structured social whole."[145] This is a clear, indisputable state of affairs which serves to support Althusser's thesis concerning the scientific impossibility of reflection on the sequence of history. Althusser writes:

Marx does not only deny us the ability to delve down beneath the complex whole (and this denial is a denial in principle: it is not ignorance which prevents us, but the very essence of production itself, its concept): Marx . . . also demonstrates . . . far from being original . . . simplicity is merely the product of a complex process . . . the simple only ever exists within a complex structure; the universal existence of a simple category . . . only appears as the end result of a long historical process.[146]

Let us not be impressed by this. Althusser has nothing to report concerning the "long historical process" other than that it must have taken place. However, the fact that should be explained is how a "simple category" such as production (or, even more importantly, labor) attains such extensive significance in a social whole. As for the whole itself, we are supposed not to be able to pose questions concerning its genesis. Rather, according to Althusser, we have before us an "ever pregivenness" as far as "knowledge delves into its past."[147] History thereby (in spite of many assurances to the contrary) is, for all practical purposes, excluded. In place of a dialectical totality steps a totalism as rigid as it is lacking in content.[148] It remains a mystery how Althusser, in view of such premises, wants to conceive of historical development, continuity, and explosive transitions. In his "Spinozaism of social forms," time appears to forfeit "every relation to the before and after, to linearity."[149]

Althusser never tires of referring to Marx's statement that exchange value as the "simplest economic category . . . can never exist other than as an abstract, one-sided relation within an already given, concrete, living whole."[150] But at the same time he neglects to observe that here Marx is not putting forth an atemporal, methodological canon but rather is observing the economic structure of bourgeois society. Marx is concerned with the "presentation"—which is model-like and removed unmediated empirical material—of his subject matter and knows very well that as a result the question concerning the "relationship between scientific presentation and the real movement"[151] of history was not settled. On the contrary, it called for more careful discussion. Marx (this is the core of materialist epistemology) specifically explains that the point is to differentiate the "totality as it appears in the head, as a totality of thoughts"[152]—following Hegel he calls it "a concrete in the mind"[153] (*ein geistig Konkretes*)—from the world itself as a *real* concrete phenomenon, whose own "process of coming into being"[154] may not be forgotten. Althusser, following this differentiation, correctly sees that the theorist always remains bound to the conceptually mediated present (as the already-present totality) and cannot arbitrarily step out of his own constructions. But he falls into speculative idealism (the very same which he so vociferously attacks) if he wants to derive from this the idea that it is scientific to start out from the eternal presence of a logically defined totality, because what distinguishes a constructed object from the real (that is, historical) object can be articulated only within present thought, and thus is a merely illusory difference.

Marx handles this problem more adequately. He knows that which Althusser firmly adheres to: that the specific role of so-called simple categories is possible only in the sphere of a totality filled with presuppositions. Nevertheless he opens up the question whether "these simpler categories also have an independent historical or natural existence predating the more concrete ones"[155]—in other words, whether they themselves are not also constitutive for the totality, to which they, in turn, owe their characteristics. This is the case to the degree to which

the simple categories are the expressions of relations within which the less developed concrete may have already realized itself before having posited the more many-sided connection or relation which is mentally expressed in the more concrete category; while the more developed concrete preserves the same category as a subordinate relation.[156]

Commodity production and money are historically possible before wage labor, capital, and banks exist. Therefore "the simpler category can express the dominant relations of a less developed whole or else those subordinate relations of a more developed whole"[157] which existed historically before the totality had developed to the point where it required a more concrete categorial structure. In this certainly special sense, "the path of abstract thought, rising from the simple to the combined, would correspond to the real historical process."[158]

The categorial expression of the relations of production investigated by Marx rested, in a mediated and/or unmediated sense, on their history. To the extent to which the thinking process is autonomous in relation to its subject matter and does not slavishly copy it, it leads to theoretical construction. Further, to the extent to which this process remains objectively related to the material of history (and continuously subjects itself to its control so as not to ossify into an empty "system"), it approaches the level of a critical historiography. Both aspects, relative independence and dependence of the thinking process vis-à-vis the historical basis, belong together. As Marx indicates, the fact that at times it appears that they have nothing to do with one another was due to the difference between the "mode of presentation" (*Darstellungsweise*) and the "mode of inquiry" (*Forschungsweise*):

The research has to appropriate the material in detail, to analyze its different forms of development and to track down their inner connection. Only after this work has been done can the real work be appropriately presented. If this is done successfully, if the life of the subject matter is now reflected back in the ideas, then it may appear as if we have before us an a priori construction.[159]

Whoever has established clarity concerning the objectively contradictory relationship between history and "system" in *Capital* will not fuse, identify, or separate the historical and the logical but rather will seek to determine the weight and place of these moments in accordance with the level then attained by the cognitive process. This is certainly a difficult task, and it is one which the structuralist Marxologists hardly pose, not to mention solve. Althusser's interpretation, which violently divides Marx's work into two heterogeneous parts, does not only sacrifice material history to theoretically constructed history. That is justified on technical grounds and is, within specified limits, unavoidable. However, it signifies an ontological regression because it dispenses with the fundamental insight into the historicity of natural and human-social existence.

Gramsci's Absolute Humanism of History

When Althusser and his students disparagingly speak of historicism, they have in mind authors like Lukács, Sartre, and Lefebvre. Of course, the tendency of Marx interpretation which they reject as ideological already existed in optimal form in Gramsci, whom Althusser had dealt with more closely (characteristically under the heading of "leftism").[160] Gramsci, an equally sharp as intelligent critic of Bukharin's "mechanism," was influenced by the neo-Hegelianism of his time.[161] Further, in a manner similar to Lukács's formulations in *History and Class Consciousness*, he characterized Marxist theory as an "absolute historicism . . . , absolute humanism of history" and also as the "philosophy of praxis." For Gramsci, speculative knowledge (as defined in the section on Feuerbach in *The German Ideology*) dissolves into real history and into historiography.[162] This corresponds to his "immanent" and extreme "subjectivist" conception of reality (one in many respects reminiscent of Bogdanov), which he reduced to "pure history or historicity and to pure humanism."[163] For Gramsci, it was particularly important to define the concept of structure, which has been formalized often enough by bourgeois (and Marxist) sociologists, in relation to its contents, that is, in a radical, historical manner, "as the ensemble of social relations, in which real individuals act and move, as an ensemble of objective conditions which can and should be studied with the methods of philology and not speculation."[164]

The Categories and Laws of Materialist Economics

According to Gramsci, Marxism, understood as a "philosophy of praxis," does justice to its revolutionary task only when it develops a "general methodology of history."[165] However, because the wealth and multiplicity of the historical process defy every barren, classificatory schema draped over phenomena and because general "laws of tendency" can be derived only to the extent to which "particular facts in their unique and unrepeatable individuality can be ascertained and specified,"[166] such a methodology calls for a sharpened philological-critical instrument.

Conversely—this complicates the issue—there is no continuum between the laws of movement of the social totality derived from earlier research and critical insight and laws based on contemporary empirical material and method. This is the case not only because, from a historical perspective, we are dealing with scarcely compatible phenomena. The categories and laws of materialist economics (regardless of their claims to objectivity) do not express the relations of production of the nineteenth century in an unmediated, or extensive manner. That would be impossible. Rather they do so in a mediated fashion through slices of abstraction—that is, as an intensive totality. Marx himself emphasizes that as these relations become scientifically fixed, they become poorer in definition and lose their historical multiplicity and consequently their "external," "accidental," and "inessential" moments as well, which are important in praxis. Marx writes in the third volume of *Capital*, "In a general analysis of this kind it is usually always assumed that the actual conditions correspond to their conception, or what is the same, that actual conditions are represented only to the extent that they are typical of their own general case." [167] Analyses directed at the particular and individual do not, as a result, become superfluous. Quite the contrary. Important theorists of political economy were always well versed in their own areas of specialization. Nevertheless, it should be kept in mind that empirically or historically attained findings are unable, at least in an unmediated sense, to shake or confirm statements concerning the social totality.

It is equally unacceptable to postulate dogmatically a total knowledge that is simply immune from revision in light of newly emergent facts. In Hegel's words, "The realm of laws is the *stable* image of the world of Existence or Appearance. [In it is expressed] the *stable* content of Appearance; . . . Appearance is the same content but presenting itself in restless flux and as reflection-into-other." [168] Materialistically interpreted, this means (analogous to the category of quantity in the Logic of Being) that within a specifiable range of variation, the essence (law) remains indifferent vis-à-vis the concrete-historical mode of its appearance. Its concept reflects the relatively constant, massive, self-repeating elements in the processes of objective reality.[169] If the essence must appear, its content consists of the conceptualized content of the appearances. Hence changes in these appearances extend to the essence itself. One problematic which forms the background of the contemporary discussion is whether capitalism since Marx and Lenin has changed essentially or only inessentially—that is, whether it manifests itself today in economic appearances whose essence is qualitatively different from the one Marx revealed. The category of a relative immiseration of the Western proletariat testifies to the difficulties that emerge in connection with this problematic.

Gramsci's Concept of Historiography

Let us return to Gramsci's problematic. He had in mind less the constructive concept of history of *Capital* than a historiography which, without degenerating into a spiritless chronicle, conformed to historical sequence and would thereby not sacrifice the specificity and nonrepeatability of individual persons and events to abstract-sociological laws. Even if one disregards for the moment the assumption that the facts of historical development are absolutely singular or theory free and are accessible only through intuition (a typical prejudice of the human sciences), a problem nevertheless does exist. History, whether constructed or described by political economy, has a different significance for the latter than it does for historical scholarship. The question concerning the relationship of general, overarching structures to particular and individual facts presents itself differently in the two cases. In the first volume of *Capital*, Marx investigates the production of relative surplus value and traces the recent history of industry since the late Middle Ages under the headings "Cooperation," "Division of Labor and Manufacture," and "Machinery and Large-scale Industry." In so doing, it is clear to him from the beginning that he is dealing with a highly generalized material, which he subjects to a selective procedure. In his "historical sketches,"[170] he presents only "broad and general characteristics, for epochs in the history of society are no more separated from each other by strict and abstract lines of demarcation than are geological epochs."[171] In other words, in *Capital*, Marx constructs not only the "economic structure" of the society he presents (capitalism) but the development of historical forms in relation to one another as well.

Historiography, by comparison, operates on a less elevated level of abstraction. As Gramsci puts it, it calls for a philological method, which takes the concrete content of individual facts into account. If Marxism is reduced to "abstract sociology"— Gramsci criticizes Bukharin's *Theory of Historical Materialism* on precisely these grounds—"a mechanical formula" would emerge "which gives the impression of holding the whole of history in the palm of its hand."[172] In fact, Bukharin does characterize Marxist materialism as sociology and the latter as "the most general [abstract] of the social sciences."[173] It takes its material from and provides a method for history. On the other hand, Bukharin separates sociology, understood in this sense, from the contents of economics and history. He defines it as "the general theory of society and the laws of its evolution."[174] Without a doubt, material history is thereby devalued, for it faces a theory which is an already closed system of coordinates in which its facts are merely registered. Bukharin does not discuss the opposite, and decisive, idea: that the historical process is constitutive for the theoretical process and modifies its categories,[175] just as he completely breaks down when it came to the dialectic (which he, following Bogdanov, replaced through a kind of equilibrium theory).

It is no wonder that Bukharin errs also on the question of the structural elements of Marxism, a question which does not co-incide with the issue of the historical sources of these elements but rather refers to the qualitatively new aspects of their theo-retical content. It was precisely this which Bukharin did not grasp. Gramsci rightly objects that Bukharin mechanistically dissects Marxism into two component parts: into a theory of evolution appearing as sociology, which works according to natural scientific criteria and (as in some contemporary authors) leads to an empty typology of historical forms; and into a phi-losophy in the narrow sense, which amounts to a crude materi-alism (falsely presenting itself as "dialectical").[176] Concerning this separation, Gramsci writes, "Separated from the theory of history and politics, philosophy cannot be other than metaphys-ics, whereas the great conquest in the history of modern thought, represented by the philosophy of praxis, is precisely the concrete historicization of philosophy and its identification with history."[177]

Gramsci as a Critic of Croce

The above offers the outlines of Gramsci's position but does not extend beyond a programmatic draft. He calls for a "science of dialectics or the theory of knowledge, within which the general concepts of history, politics and economics are interwoven in an organic unity."[178] Elsewhere Gramsci formulates this idea more precisely. He criticizes Croce's thought because it calls for the "identity of history and philosophy" but only in order to reduce history to "ethical-political history," that is, to superstructural phenomena.[179] Its full meaning attains such an identity only when it also leads to an identity of history and politics (by "poli-tics" must be understood self-realizing politics and not the re-peated attempts at realizations, of which some will fail) and consequently to an identity of politics and philosophy. If the politician is a historian (not only in the sense that he makes history but also that he interprets the past while acting in the present) so the historian is a politician. And in this sense history is always contemporary history, that is, politics.[180] This is a serious consequence, one that Croce's radical historicism does not challenge. Indeed, he claims to have expunged all transcendental, theological, and traditional-metaphysical remnants from his thinking. But Gramsci convincingly points out that Croce does not fulfill this claim and that his philosophy remains embedded in the speculative: "In it is contained the whole transcendance and theology scarcely freed from the crudest mythological wrappings."[181]

Gramsci discusses the stance of political moderation expressed in Croce's historical thought and surmises that it is to be explained by national particularities, in particular by the "historical fact of the absence of a unified people's initiative within Italian history."[182] Its course creates, as Gramsci showed, among the bourgeois intellectuals a remarkable ideology which shifts back and forth between revolution and restoration. In Italy this development took place essentially as a reaction by the dominant class to the spontaneous, disorganized revolts of the masses of the people. The ensuing "restorations" fulfilled certain demands of the proletariat and were, in his words, "progressive restorations" or "passive revolutions."[183] Croce's historicism thus mixes liberal and conservative elements in such a way that the only political activity permissible is that which contributes to progress by way of the "dialectic of preservation and renewal."[184] As a Hegelian, Gramsci endorses this view, which claims that in the historically new, the old is always rejected and retained. In Croce, however, this principle becomes ideological, a "mere reflex of a practical-political tendency"[185] and does so to the extent that he, in a rather arbitrary and a priori manner, believes he can ordain what must be preserved and set aside. Croce, like all other liberal reformers, advocates "a cleverly masked form of predesigned history"[186] under the illusion of a consciousness sharpened by history. What presents itself as pure contemplation of the Heraclitean river, is, in truth, an interest-bound class standpoint. This standpoint is evident less in unmediated reactionary content than in the form and method of its emergence. Hegel's "negativity" loses its salt in Croce's ideology, for the latter tends, in Gramsci's view, "to ennervate the antitheses, to parcel them out into a long chain of isolated moments . . . and to reduce the dialectic to a process of reformist evolution, a process of 'revolution-restoration,' in which only the second term is effective and valid."[187] By contrast, it is indicative of Gramsci's scientific historicism that it remains open to the objectivity of the process. It cannot prejudge which moments from the enormous complex of the past will be preserved in a future condition (although its consciousness must be appropriate to the level attained by the history of the human species and have at its disposal a measure of desired values which themselves are immanent to history). Whatever moves from the past into the future, Gramsci writes, "will bear the character of historical necessity and not that of the accidental choice by so-called scholars and philosophers."[188]

Gramsci claims to fulfill the neo-Hegelian program of a strictly "immanentist conception of reality" by tracing it back to "pure history or historicity and to pure humanism."[189] This project, however, is not a concession to a static anthropology. At no point does Gramsci neglect "historicist or realist immanence."[190] The "philosophy of praxis," as the most complete expression of historical contradictions, rejects the hypothesis of invariant structures: "'Man in general,' in whatever form he presents himself, is denied and all dogmatically 'unitary' concepts are spurned and destroyed as expressions of the concept of 'man in general' or of 'human nature' immanent in every man."[191] In this fundamental aspect of his thought, Gramsci sees that the heritage of classical German philosophy (of course, mediated by modern history) is preserved in Marx.

I have discussed Gramsci's critique of Bukharin's naive ontology (it explains the much exaggerated "subjectivist" accent of Gramsci's epistemological considerations)[192] and of Italian neo-Hegelianism (and its reception of Marx) because the representatives of the Althusser school think of Gramsci, above all, when they talk of historicist misinterpretations of Marxism. Clearly Gramsci, who was largely unknown in postwar West Germany, has exercised a considerable influence on French intellectuals since the war. The Parisians are particularly critical of what Gramsci occasionally said about Marx's relationship to classical economics, and, in fact, the limits of Gramsci's scientific-theoretical project become apparent in these comments. The identification of the theory of knowledge with historicism and of philosophy with the writing of history, which Gramsci takes over from Croce,[193] may in part stand the test of Marx's early writings (as well as of his historical writings in the narrow sense of the word). But it contributes hardly anything, especially in an inner economic sense, to the contemporary problematic of *Capital*, which is at issue today.

Nevertheless it pays to dwell on this for a while because it concerns the core of dialectical materialism. Although his concepts may remain characteristically "experimental" and "atmospheric,"[194] Gramsci, along with Lukács and Korsch, was among the most meritorious of the authors who intentionally reached back to Hegel's dialectic in the 1920s and early 1930s and in so doing put new life into the philosophical impulse of Marxist thought, which was suffering from crude-naturalistic social-democratic as well as Soviet Russian orthodoxy. (This was accomplished, however, at the price of a more or less serious idealist relapse.) What has sometimes been interpreted as Gramsci's intellectual incoherence—the "floating" (*Schwebende*) of his categories—is really due to the fact that he was schooled in Hegel and thus guarded against assumptions contrary to history and kept in view the character of truth as a process.

Gramsci on the Scientific-Theoretical Status of Marxist Theory

Shifting once again to the discussion of Althusserian structuralism, let us turn to the political-economic aspects of Gramsci's reflections. Although open to question in particulars, they also contain essential moments of a critical interpretation of Marx, one going beyond an interpretation that merely serves as a confessional world view.

Gramsci criticizes the "mechanistic" materialism which he first saw at work not in Bukharin but rather in the "revisionist" Social Democracy of the prewar era. Bernstein's famous remark—the movement is everything, the end goal nothing—replaced the historical dialectic with mechanics. In the Marxism of the Second International, Marx's comments in the *Theses on Feuerbach* fell into oblivion: "Human power was viewed as passive and unconscious, as an element indistinguishable from material things. The vulgar, naturalistically interpreted concept of evolution displaced the concept of development."[195] To the extent that the revisionists theoretically allowed for human intervention in the iron course of events, it entered as the "thesis or moment of resistance and conservation [not as] the antithesis or . . . initiative . . . , which, in order to strengthen its transcending movement, presupposes the awakening of latent, bold, stimulating forces and requires the positing of immediate and intermediate goals."[196]

This is a thoroughly justified critique and is one which embroiled Gramsci in the difficult and oft-posed question of how the scientific-theoretical status of Marx's lifework was to be evaluated. In order to answer it, Gramsci recalls Lenin's 1913 essay *Three Sources and Three Component Parts of Marxism*. Speaking of Marx, Lenin wrote that "his theory emerged as the direct and immediate continuation of the teachings of the greatest representatives of philosophy, political economy and socialism. . . .

It is the legitimate successor to the best that man produced in the nineteenth century, as represented by German philosophy, English political economy and French socialism."[197] But this does not yet explain the mode in which "these three cultural movements,"[198] as Gramsci puts it enter Marx's conceptual structure. Given that this structure "synthesized . . . the entire culture of the age,"[199] all three sources must reappear in it as anticipatory moments. It is this reemergence of the anticipatory moments which guides Gramsci. He further speculates that the "unitary moment of synthesis [of Marxism] is to be identified in the new concept of immanence, which has been translated from the speculative form, as put forward by classical German philosophy, into a historicist form with the aid of French politics and English classical economics."[200]

Gramsci's Interpretation of the Relationship of Historical Materialism to the Critique of Political Economy

Gramsci proposes to examine systematically the relationship among philosophical, economic, and political elements in Marx. He writes that "in a sense . . . the philosophy of praxis equals Hegel plus David Ricardo,"[201] a thesis that should be understood as a substantive rather than an external-genetic one. It raises the question as to whether the principles which Ricardo introduced into economics exhaust themselves in their instrumental function or if they (although first of all conceived according to formal logic) signify a substantive-philosophical novum. To pose the question in this manner is to answer it in the affirmative. This is not to say that Gramsci's fleeting notes master the problem of the transition from Ricardo to Marx. But unlike the structuralist interpretations, they pose the issue in a more appropriate manner. Gramsci recognizes that the objective possibility of discovering "tendential laws" appeared for the first time in Ricardo and that this possibility encompassed a qualitatively new conception of immanence, necessity, and freedom. This conception is developed by Marxism, which, as Gramsci writes, "universalized Ricardo's discoveries, extending them in an adequate form to the whole of history."[202]

Gramsci's particular interest is devoted to the dialectical reformulation of the concept of law, a reformulation initiated by Ricardo's economics. Once again, taking *The German Ideology* as his starting point, Gramsci makes reference to the modern bourgeois origins of economic scholarship. He argues that to the degree to which the bourgeoisie attains the level of universal activity and a "world market" develops as a "nature-like form of the world-historical co-operation of individuals,"[203] which stands over against them as an alien power, it is "possible to isolate and study necessary laws of regularity."[204] Gramsci immediately adds that "these are laws of tendency, which are not laws in the naturalistic sense or that of speculative determinism . . . but [are] in a 'historicist' sense valid, that is, to the extent that there exists the 'determined market' or, in other words, an environment which is organically alive."[205] This insight remains closed to Ricardo. His method considers these laws only as a "quantitative expression of phenomena."[206] In other words, it remains within the horizon of bourgeois thought. This horizon is transcended by the Marxist "passage from economics to general history" in which for the sake of enriching the concept of law, "the concept of quantity is integrated with that of quality."[207]

For Gramsci, a theoretical and actual change in the relationship between freedom and necessity accompanies the integration of qualitative moments. (This integration marks the break with classical economics. To necessity corresponds the predominance of quantity, to freedom that of quality. The former characterizes the hitherto existing nature-like quality of historical processes, the latter the task of human beings of learning to control the social forms of their domination of nature. The well-known thesis of Engels's *Anti-Dühring*, that "historical development will at a certain point be characterized by the passage from the reign of necessity to the reign of freedom,"[208] means, when carefully considered, that Marxism puts forward no claim for eternal validity but rather must be understood as the conceptual and conscious expression of conditions whose transitoriness it has, at least in principle, perceived. Irrefutable prognosis cannot be derived from it. However, as long as these conditions (which are not controlled by the individuals who produce them) persist, the materialist theory is associated with necessity rather than with the not-yet-existent freedom

Gramsci writes, "At the present time, the philosopher—the philosopher of praxis— . . . cannot escape from the present field of contradictions; he cannot affirm, other than generically, a world without contradictions without immediately creating a utopia."[209] Due to its abstractness, this utopia may be of minimal philosophical or even political value. It is, however, by all means preferable to the fetishized service to naked factuality widely fostered not only by bourgeois but also by vulgar Marxist thought. Here Gramsci has in mind representatives of an unmediated objectivism such as Kautsky and Bukharin, who helped to disseminate a corresponding interpretation of Marxist theory in the enemy camp. His reflections on the law-like nature of historical development are sufficiently remarkable to merit further comment.

Gramsci thinks it improbable that Marx borrowed the historical-theoretical categories of "regularity" and "necessity" directly from the natural sciences.[210] Rather, in this view they originate from (and here Gramsci is adopting important themes especially from the late Engels) "the terrain of political economy, particularly in the form and with the methodology that economic science acquired from David Ricardo."[211] Classical economics attained the insight, Gramsci continues, that the operation of decisive and permanent forces presents itself with a certain "automatism" which allows a measure of "predictability" and certainty for the future of those individual initiatives which accept these forces. . . . After having established . . . the spontaneous automatism of these forces (i.e., their relative independence from individual choices and from arbitrary government interventions) the economist has, by way of hypothesis, rendered the automatism absolute; he has isolated the merely economic facts from the combinations of varying importance . . . and he has thus produced an abstract scheme of a determined economic society. (On this realistic construct there has subsequently been imposed an . . . abstraction of "man" as such, an "ahistorical" abstraction . . . that has come to be seen as "true" economic science.)[212]

This is Gramsci's rather sketchy but essentially correct presentation of the political-economic premises of Marxist historical thought that often appear in textbooks. Gramsci sees that the mechanics of the market, as well as social-phenomenal forms in general "which present themselves as something 'objective,' comparable to the automatism of natural phenomena,"[213] are mediated on a subjective level, through individual self-conscious acts which, however, are unconscious in relation to the social total result to which they contribute. Gramsci stresses that what the bourgeois economists called eternal and natural reveals itself, when subjected to Marxist critique, to be transitory and man-made. In his view, this critique, when considering the structures of society, does not fail to grasp the activity of individuals who created these structures.

In the following, I will briefly summarize those aspects of Gramsci's "absolute historicism" which are central to the contemporary discussion of the Marxist concept of history. Although up to this point in my argument I have devoted hardly any attention to the fact, these aspects belong substantively within the scope of the critical theory conceived in the 1930s by Horkheimer, Adorno, and Marcuse.

1. Philosophy, politics, and economics are "sources and components" (Lenin) of Marx's work, which constitute its inner unity and hence are transferable and translatable into one another. Philosophical discourse is always simultaneously political and economic discourse and vice-versa (without thereby having the layers of meaning becoming arbitrarily confused). Together they form a "homogeneous circle."[214] This Gramscian insight is important from an interpretative perspective because among other things it warns against seeking out the philosophical element in Marx only where he made use of the conventional language of philosophy. Often (this applies mutatis mutandis to Lenin or Mao Tse-tung as well) Marx's historical-political writings contain more compelling philosophical aspects than do those works specifically dealing with philosophical themes.[215]

2. In refusing to isolate the epistemological problematic of the materialist conception of history from the substantive questions of Marxist economics, Gramsci follows authentic Marxist theory. Thus, in his formulations, talk of the "dependence" (*Bedingtheit*) of different forms of consciousness on social being loses the character which adheres to it in numerous official party presentations, that is, the character of an unproven ontological thesis. Such presentations often give the impression that the Marxist critique of political economy amounts to a simple application of a completed, closed philosophy to an equally complete, closed, and pregiven special domain. Such a view suppresses two points. First, Marx was able to develop philosophically (especially epistemologically) decisive categories above all in terms of economic contents, whose historical-social determination he had penetrated. Second, his critical incorporation of Hegelian motifs was in no sense restricted to his early writings but rather reemerged anew precisely after 1850 on a sharper conceptual plane.[216]

3. Gramsci's notes point to the often-neglected inner connection between historical materialism and economic critique but

do not investigate this connection in detail. Nevertheless, Gramsci touches on the nerve of Marxist theory when he attempts to trace the domination of objective forces over individuals, that is, of being over consciousness back to the uncontrolled rule of the law of value in prehistory, a rule at whose end, as Gramsci emphasizes, socialist theory aims. His negative interpretation, therefore, is of considerable interest because it undermines the still-current view according to which Marx is said to have been unreflectively bound "to natural scientific, one could say: nomological conceptions of laws,"[217] which appear as quasi-religious guarantees of salvation. What Marx criticizes in the world of commodity fetishism—that in it what is a social creation is venerated as an autonomous being-in-itself to whose rigid objectivity individuals submit—is elevated by this view (one widespread among ostensible adherents of Marxism) into a scientific norm. In contrast, Adorno, in *Negative Dialectics*, explicitly emphasizes that here, as in all dialectical matters, the mediation passes through the extremes. Being as product (*Erzeugt-sein*) and being-in-itself (*An-Sich*) of what Marx calls "societal natural laws" are complementary as abstractly divided moments. As Adorno writes, "The thesis that society is subject to natural laws is ideology if it is hypostasized as immutably given by nature. But this legality is real as a law of motion for the unconscious society."[218] For Adorno, Marx's unfolding of this law with a view toward its future abolition constitutes the "strongest motif"[219] of Marx's conception.

Gramsci's unbroken identification of history and theory, his idea of "pure" process and praxis (meaning that the future is absolutely subject to human influence), and the related establishment of the primacy of the subject in Fichte's sense[220] had to bring down on him the structuralist accusation of naive historicism. In the following section I will once again explain what is important in this critique, one that neglects Gramsci's impulse, which, in spite of its faults, is a great one. In principle, this critique does not spare Marx's work itself from similar criticism. The level that the discussion has now attained allows new aspects to be brought to bear on the problem.

Difficulties of Marx Interpretation

Aside from Althusser's *For Marx* and Poulantzas's works, *Reading Capital* remains the most reliable source of the structuralist interpretation of Marx. In 1968, Althusser and Balibar published a new edition of both volumes in a tighter and pithier form.[221] In the foreword to that edition, Althusser objected that, almost without exception the conceptions of his school had been judged to be a variety of structuralism. In spite of terminological similarities in particulars and in spite of certain ambiguities, Althusser claims that the "profound tendency" of his own theoretical efforts is to be sharply distinguished from every "structuralist ideology."[222] He insists that the concept of combination present in his work has nothing in common with the customary structuralist notion of a "combinatory," not to mention other of his categories such as the primacy of the economic, domination, overdetermination, or production process. This protestation is hardly satisfactory, for it dogmatically presupposes that only Althusserianism has put forward an appropriate Marx exegesis. What this exegesis claims for itself—that its true tendency will not be adversely affected by the terminology in which it is expressed—is supposed to be yet truer of Marx himself. Of course a careful interpreter will be on guard against a naive reading of the texts. As with other authors of his stature, the material results of Marx's work do not (or only partially) coincide with what he occasionally presents as a fixed self-understanding in his politically consequential, oft-cited forewords. Furthermore a complex work such as Marx's can be unfolded only successively. New aspects of the work which have been neglected previously reveal themselves to the degree to which the theoretical (and practical) need emerges to discover them. For example, such previously unknown·features of Marx's work have become clear in the medium of Kantian, Hegelian, and even existentialist interpretation (in spite of the exaggerations present in such analyses). Of course a similar role devolves on the most recent structuralist Marx interpretations as well. However, the fact that the exponents of this interpretation are not satisfied with this circumscribed role and instead wish to put forth a "completely new" Marx connects them to the search for glory of those previous efforts.

To be sure, faced with the structuralist interpretation—and this is what we have in spite of claims to the contrary—special caution is required. The ever-changing history of Marx interpretation points to the conclusion that whenever the so-called letter was sacrificed to the spirit, it was the former that suffered the damage. The worst Stalinist deformations of Marxist theory took place in the name of a critique of Talmudists and bookworms. Althusser's method is not free from traces of this harmful and unfortunate tradition. He does not interpret (or does so only infrequently) familiar Marxist ideas in structuralist language. (Such an interpretation would certainly serve to illuminate it.) Rather he presents structuralist positions without ceremony as Marxist ones. This is especially applicable to a concept as fundamental to *Capital* as that of history.

Capital in the Optics of the Old Social Democracy

Before we enter this problematic in depth, it is useful to glance at the history of the reception of Marx's major work during the nineteenth century.[223] Only by doing so can one do justice to the structuralist reinterpretation of Marx.

In addition to bourgeois scholars, such as Lamprecht, Schmoller, Max Weber, and Sombart, who tried to use particular elements of Marxist method in their studies in economic and social history, important theorists of the Second International also defended the thesis that Marx's merit was primarily of a historiographical nature. For example, Kautsky saw in *Capital* an "essentially historical work . . . [a] new historical and economic system."[224] Mehring, following Kautsky, argued that *Capital* "in reference to history" is like "a mine whose treasure has remained largely unexcavated."[225] In 1893, as Mehring wrote these lines, Marx's lifework as a whole was grounded in historical materialism. (Engels's well-known letters display a similar emphasis.) In the world of official scholarship, the importance of historical materialism for a scientific historiography was hardly acknowledged, not to mention understood or recognized. (Of course even today such recognition is still rare.) In the old Social Democracy, a dual task fell to Mehring (along with Kautsky) as a historian and literary scholar: to test the materialist method on concrete material and to refute the view common among bourgeois scholars that Marx and Engels had "only here and there taken a detour into historical scholarship . . . in order to support a theory of history they had invented."[226]

Althusser's Reinterpretation

The authors of the Second International grasped the constitutive role of history for Marx and Engels's conceptual framework. They were also particularly aware of the presence of historical thought in *Capital*. But how this occurred, how historical and structural-analytic elements were related to one another, remained beyond their grasp. The indisputable service that the Althusser school has performed consists of having energetically pointed to the difficulty present in this issue. Its representatives belong to a postexistentialist generation, which—tired of the empty cult of the "young Marx"[227]—has initiated an extremely intensive study of critical political economy, which aims at conceptual rigor and scientific objectivity. In principle this would be most welcome if such rigor did not have as its consequence the rejection of crucial aspects of the Marxist conception as "ideological" in the name of a standpoint which understands itself theoretically as "antihumanism" and "antihistoricism." As a result, the interest in a more humane society remains a moral postulate that is both external to and ungrounded in the actual theoretical process.[228] I have already addressed this issue in this study and elsewhere.[229] Now the point is to confront the structuralist Marx interpretation with the texts themselves.

For a long time, it has been assumed in Marxist literature that in *Capital*, as Lenin said (and his view represents that of numerous authors), Marx provided a "theoretical and historical analysis"[230] of bourgeois society. Indeed Lenin saw that the "and" of this quote was important. He argued that a break between the "abstract theory of capitalism,"[231] which refers to its fully developed form, and history will develop to the degree to which such a theory neglects the aspect of the genesis of this fully developed form. (Marx developed this thought in the rough draft of *Capital*, the *Grundrisse*.) Lenin also emphasized that orthodoxy does not permit "historical problems to be obscured by abstract schemes"[232] taken from intellectual constructs in an unmediated manner. Lenin called for a particular kind of study in which "abstract-theoretical" questions would not be confused with "concrete-historical"[233] ones, although the former must spring from the historical world if such a study is to be conceptualized in a materialist framework.

The Philosophy of the "Nouvel Esprit Scientifique": Epistemology as Constructed History of Science

The break between theory and history to which Lenin referred forms the starting point for structuralist Marx interpreters. Of course Marxist structuralists cannot in any sense claim to be the only ones to have discovered and considered this anything-but-academic problematic.[234] But they present it in such a radical form that a premature harmonization of theory and history is ruled out from the beginning. (In the most abstract sense, such a harmonization is correct, but, precisely because of this level of abstraction, it contributes little or nothing to a solution of the break.)

Understanding the Althusserian undertaking requires that we consider the intellectual climate in which it could emerge. Althusser leaves no doubt that he owes a great deal to authors such as Bachelard, Cavailles, Canguilhem, and Foucault, all of whom had sought to establish an epistemology grounded in a history of science. In particular, they raised the question concerning the gnoseological content of what is usually, and all too innocently, called "scientific progress." What do we mean by scientific progress? What criteria can adequately judge the transition from one theory to another? What differentiates prescientific or unscientific, or in Marxist terms, ideological concepts from scientific ones?

Bachelard, one of the most important founders of contemporary epistemology, was intensively engaged in this problem. His "philosophy of the scientific discovery"[235]—and this was supposed to have impressed structuralist authors—resisted the positivistic (especially Comtean) fusion of the history and philosophy of science.[236] In Bachelard's view, it is a historicizing laziness of thought that satisfies itself with retrospectively arranging new findings in an evolutionary schema. He claims that although traditional historical writing always tried to stay close on the heels of the sciences, it was rarely in a position to capture their real dynamic with its breaks, crises, and turning points. Imprisoned in the past, it could see in the new only improved variants of the old. Bachelard writes that it is important to fight against this "recurrent optimism which wants to place a veneer of new values on old discoveries."[237] He attributes the uneasiness between philosophers and scholars to the positivist history of science, which demands from philosophers who faithfully follow the course of discoveries that they have proof that such discoveries are determined by what came before. In contrast, Bachelard attempted to demonstrate, both historically and in a general-analytic sense, how mistaken this unreasonable demand directed at the philosophers was. Hence his comments on the emergence of Einsteinian physics: "Historically speaking, the appearance of relativist theories . . . is surprising. If there is indeed a doctrine which is not explained by historical antecedents, it is the doctrine of relativity."[238] In reference to the relation between the logical and the temporal in the cognitive process, Bachelard explains that he is decidedly opposed to naive-linear thinking about history:

It is easy to think that scientific problems succeed one another by order of increasing complexity. . . . [In taking such a view] one forgets that the solution found reflects its clarity on the given, bears schemas that simplify and direct experience, and that a partial solution fits into a general system or may be a supplementary force.[239]

Two things are decisive for Bachelard (as for his structuralist followers). First, if the history of science is to satisfy epistemological demands, it must be studied retrospectively, that is, from the viewpoint of its most advanced level. Second, the progress of knowledge does not correspond to the evolutionary principle of the transition from the simple to the complex. The theory that is "simpler," due to its being more abstract, does not exist at the beginning but rather works through previous results of thought processes and is, to that degree, the conception that is more "concrete" (in the Hegelian sense), richer in content.

It is characteristic of Bachelard, Canguilhem, and Althusser as well that their work contains merely general speculations concerning historical processes in the history of science. They allow themselves to be guided by the view that their epistemological problematic originates in specific substantive questions.[240] What is to be explained are the conditions making possible the transition from more-or-less ideologically colored words to strict concepts. This presupposes that it is wrong to view the history of science as a mere junkroom of previous errors. Such a view would be justified only on the basis of a definitive, final state of knowledge, which is impossible. All theories deal with facts that have been theoretically filtered. Hence no final judgment can be rendered on these facts. They emerge from intellectual constructions, which themselves are often older than the immediately preceding level of knowledge and originate in completely different scientific or technical areas. Epistemologists cannot allow themselves to be passively guided by external chronology.[241]

Althusser's Bachelardian Presuppositions

The concept of the "new scientific spirit"[242] that is most important for Althusser's Marx interpretation is the Bachelardian idea of a *coupure épistémologique*.[243] The latter is a notion that refers to a break (a "cut") in theory's historical development, which affects both theory's method and its object and which signifies a new problematic, a new level of scientific discourse. Bachelard emphasizes that the historian of science deals with the "paleontology of a scientific spirit that has disappeared."[244] In Bachelard's view, between contemporary science and science of the past,[245] there does not exist any sort of continuity. It is less historical phases than object domains which the epistemological break separates—for example, that of science from that of images and symbols which expose us to constant error.

The term *épistémologie* has a narrower meaning in French than does *Erkenntnistheorie* in German. The latter refers to investigations into the no-man's-land of logic, metaphysics, and psychology, which—decisively stamped by Kant—reflect on the subjective constituents of objectivity. In contrast, French linguistic usage makes a sharp distinction between *épistémologie* and *théorie de la connaissance*. The latter received only archival interest in the textbooks. The subjective impulse from Descartes to Husserl looks old-fashioned, especially in contemporary France. On the other hand, as Bachelard writes, *épistémologie* serves as a metatheoretical discipline

> whose object of study is the formation and transformation of scientific concepts, how they change from science to science, how the field of study is constituted, the rules according to which it is organized across successive mutations and how, in relation to its own rules, a practice becomes conscious of its method.[246]

This characterization makes clear that epistemological thinking does not aim at grounding the dominant form of conventional scientific practice. It presupposes it as historical material and merely would like to help it attain clear self-consciousness. The extent to which this *philosophie du nouvel esprit scientifique* departs from older positivism is apparent in Bachelard's energetic attempt to revise the idea of the history of science. Scientism, in Noiray's words, is "an unfaithful positivism" (*un positivisme infidèle*).[247] Its problematic relationship to linearly interpreted history had to expand its rationalistic-constructive features, especially in France. However, because it would step beyond the framework of this essay to discuss in greater detail the questions growing out of the discussion of scientism, we must be content with stressing particular moments which, in modified form, enter into Althusser's undertaking.[248]

Bachelard's conception of the scientifically modern is a dialectical one[249] insofar as it rejects Cartesian rationalism, which claims to be incontestable due to its immutability, in favor of an "approximate knowledge" (*connaissance approchée*). He writes, "Approximation is an incomplete objectification, but it is a prudent, fertile, truly rational one since it is conscious of the insufficiency of its progress."[250] Cognition, in other words, is not a singular, unique act or a catalog of fixed sentences. Rather it is a multifarious, ramified process. The fact that scientific rationality always remains behind the extensive and intensive infinity of the actual is not evidence of an avoidable defect of the cognitive process. Rather it demonstrates its fundamental lawfulness. Bachelard insists that reason loses the autarchy which has been rationalistically attributed to it. It has committed itself to the path of science:

Reason must obey science, the most highly evolved science, science in the process of evolution. Reason has no right to put a premium upon an immediate experience; on the contrary it must put itself in balance with the most richly structured experience. In all circumstances the immediate must yield to the constructed.[251]

On the basis of this relationship between reason and science, Bachelard develops a decidedly non-Cartesian epistemology. Its starting point is not the irreducible facts of consciousness but rather the idea that all scientific activity is subject to a historical dialectic which develops between the poles of the rational and the experimental. In the development of this dialectic, "truths of reason" work together with "truths of experience."[252] Both lose their abstract identity: the conceptual constructions manifest their relative, provisional character just as much as the descriptive results of empirical research do. Bachelard speaks of an "applied rationalism" giving a dynamic to reason, which is complemented by a "rational materialism" (epistemological realism).[253] The latter, of course, is anything but a naive sensualism: "All progress of the philosophy of science goes in the direction of a growing rationalism, eliminating . . . the initial rationalism."[254] Bachelard approaches Marx and Engels's critique of Feuerbach's contemplative thinking when he underscores to what a great extent the object of knowledge must be seen as a "manufactured object . . . [a] civilized object. The domain of the real prolongs itself into the domain of realization. It would then be easy . . . to prove that between reality and realization rational factors have intervened."[255] It is unimportant that Bachelard does not put forward a substantial concept of collective praxis (objective, concrete activity), for on an abstract, scientific level, he demonstrates the increasing impossibility of pure nature. The formerly "given" transforms itself into something "produced." The objects with which scholars are concerned are continuously developing. For example, in chemistry, substances are not studied in the form of their natural deposits. Here as well "the real" is defined as "realization."[256]

Unlike the conventional historian of science, the epistemologist of the Bachelardian school does not view historically emergent ideas as facts that are to be chronologically classified. Rather he views the facts as ideas. He assumes that everything empirical (including the research apparatus oriented to the quantitative) is always something that has been conceptually processed; it is, in Bachelard's words, "a realized theorem."[257] The scientific intellect can approach objective being (*Sein*) only by means of its own hypotheses, outlines, and concepts. To the extent to which experimentation is also an indispensable moment of the thought process (and not its aid or substitute but rather "the production of new reality"),[258] knowledge progresses from the rational to the real. Bachelard claims that our constructs, as well as the material to which they refer, are refined in this process.

Bachelard, according to one of his French interpreters, Guéry, demonstrates that a new form of thought emerges synthetically from the "dialogue" between "rationalism" and "realism." Each complements and corrects the other without denying the cognitive primacy of the rational.[259] This emphatically realist project (all conceptual mediations of the object notwithstanding) marks the essential difference between the "new rationalism"[260] and the empiricist-sensualist traditions of positivism, which, from Hume through Nietzsche up to Mach and Avenarius, rejected the thesis of the knowability of a being-in-itself. For these traditions, such a being was synonymous with an unproven metaphysics. This is an objection that apparently has been unable to shake the epistemological optimism of modern rationalists. They continue to insist on the existence of an ordered reality outside the mind. Despite their criticism of its surface structure, subjective reflection remains alien to them. Bachelard—to clarify yet again his defining influence—delivers to structural methodology not only a revised concept of the history of science, which, as did Marx, derives the past from the present; in addition, he shows how important it is to investigate science *in statu nascendi*. When Bachelard speaks of the emergence of something new, he in no sense restricts himself to sharply outlined historical caesuras (*coupures épistémologiques*) but rather points to something that is endlessly repeated: progress in general knows that death-like rigidity takes its only alternative and consists in the ceaseless struggle against it.[261] Bachelard views the whole development of science as a coherent discontinuum. In so doing, he deviates from Bergson, whose metaphysic of life and knowledge emanates from the "concrete duration" and the "moving continuity of the real."[262] Bachelard argues that at every level, methodological thinking must avoid the constant danger of falling into mere images. Here he speaks of an "epistemological obstacle" (*obstacle épistémologique*),[263] which, as Guéry stresses, cannot be understood as something external to science that can be dismissed as a side issue. Science, he writes, is far more "a pure innovation, a creation which makes its object appear only retrospectively."[264] Thus the belief in phlogiston proved to be such an obstacle only after the presentation of oxygen.

The reality with which cognition is concerned is the product of earlier activity; it is formed matter which requires further transformation. The relevance of the data on which the theory focuses is created by the theory itself. Summarizing Bachelard's conception, Guéry writes that science brings forth forms which rectify the old structures and thereby create new objects.[265] By insisting in this manner on the active, creative character of cognitive processes, Bachelard approaches not only the character of social labor but also, like Nietzsche, that of artistic production. We will now deal with the questionable aspect of this approach: its insufficient (from a Marxist standpoint) definition of activity (praxis), its identification with technology.[266]

Formalized and Material History of the Sciences

The foundation of the epistemology of modern rationalism on the basis of a new interpretation of the history of science was important for structuralist thinking about history. According to Bachelard, the advance of our knowledge does not take place in smooth transitions but rather does so suddenly, in leaps. What was previously called "development" or "becoming" now presents itself as a succession (insofar as the concept retains a genetic meaning) of "unique and novel moments."[267] Contemporary advocates and continuers of the Bachelardian (as well as Koyrésian) project who belong to Althusser's circle directly juxtapose a "position of discontinuity" to the previous "position of continuity"[268] (such as that advocated by Brunschvicg and Duhem). The latter assumes what the former denies: that there exists an immanent coherence of knowledge (as well as of the real history conditioning it) that persists throughout any stage of development. In particular, the "position of discontinuity" denies, at least by implication, the origins of scientific thinking in the prescientific life world.[269] On this view, the level of science is always attained through a break (*coupure constitutrice*) with the received problem field (*espace de problemes*),[270] a field which is ideological insofar as its concepts work with unconsciously operating images and myths.[271] The break with this ideological problematic does not mean that it will be pursued with more appropriate means. On the contrary, a new level of discourse emerges, one which does not transcend (in the Hegelian sense) the previous level but rather completely replaces it.

Of course, even the structuralist historians of science have to recognize that the forms of thought which are judged after the epistemological break to be ideological do not at all constitute a mere misty region (*Nebelregion*). Even Bachelard speaks of a web of positive, enduring errors, while the Althusserians concede that corrections and criticisms (*ruptures intra-idéologiques*)[272] exist within the lines of ideological demarcation. Further, they admit the great extent to which the primarily philosophical ideologies that precede science prepare its ground. The ideological prehistory of every science, the Althusserians claim, is a "process of accumulation . . . the period of formation of the conjuncture in which the break is produced."[273] This concession, however, does not mean that the structuralists are, along with Marx, convinced of the correctness of the Hegelian law "that at a certain point merely quantitative differences pass over by a dialectical inversion into qualitative distinctions."[274] Instead they stress how much the particular breakthrough toward a specific scientific problematic rests on the statements of the problem that precedes it. But they refuse to view these error-ridden, largely tentative efforts as constitutive for the form of new initiatives that go beyond them. On the other hand, Hegel's concept of the "nodal line of measure-relations,"[275] which entered into dialectical materialism, presupposes that "progressive gradualness" and explosive transition "from a quantitative into a qualitative alteration"[276] form a contradiction (the "quantitative progress . . . is absolutely interrupted")[277] without, thereby, setting aside the general unity of the movement, that is, of the "substrate with itself."[278] For Hegel, just the opposite is the case. He emphasizes how mistaken it is to conceive of the emergence of new qualities as if this process could be traced back to a general notion of emergence and decline. Rather, in Hegel's view, the new springs from the sudden "interruption of gradualness,"[279] which paradoxically produces linear development. As Hegel said, "The substrate continues itself into this differentiation."[280]

Continuity and discontinuity—Hegel prefers the term *discretion*—form a dialectical unity insofar as neither, continuity as little as discretion, can claim truth when taken separately. Both categories, moments of quantity, have meanings that reciprocally refer to one another. In Hegel's words, "Continuity is only coherent, compact unity as unity of the discrete."[281]

Here Hegel's reflections on the logic of being are of considerable utility not only because they throw light on Bachelard's and Althusser's problem of the emergence of new theories (or theorems) from old theories in the course of the history of science,[282] but also, and more importantly, because they illuminate the problem of history in general.

Concerning the problem of the emergence of new theories, the structuralist efforts to solve it are not at all new. Aspects of their work which we find acceptable are already to be found in the work of authors who today are accused of engaging in historical-philosophical speculation: Comte, Marx, and Hegel.

Comte, Hegel, and Marx as Historians of Science

Comte, in the second lecture of the *Cours de Philosophie positive* (1826), which advanced general considerations on the hierarchy of the sciences, discussed the question (which was an important one for Marx) of the mode of presentation (*mode d'exposition*).[283] He maintained that every science can be presented according to two essentially different modes and that all further efforts amount to their mere combination. These two modes were, Comte claimed, the historical and the dogmatic form of presentation (*Darstellungweise*). The former (*la marche historique*) presents its finding sequentially, that is, as closely as possible in accordance with their actual occurrences in the human spirit. The latter (*la marche dogmatique*) develops a system of ideas which can be conceptualized today by the individual scholar striving to represent science from an appropriate standpoint as a differentiated whole. The research of every newly emergent science begins with the historical method; its didactics must be confined to treating different works in the chronological sequence in which they made their contributions to scientific progress. By contrast, the dogmatic procedure is one that is little concerned with chronology. It assumes that particular works are already woven into a general system and that they can only be presented in a logical order (Comte called it a "more natural" order) in the context of this system. Such presentation, in turn, requires a high level of development of the discipline in question. The more differentiated a science is, the less it can be historically depicted; those occupied with it would have to go through an immense chain of intermediate links. This is not the case with the dogmatic method. In Comte's view, it increasingly recommends itself because new theoretical conceptions arise that are able to present previous discoveries under more direct viewpoints. Thus he spoke of a "permanent tendency of the human spirit, concerning the exposition of consciousness . . . to increasingly substitute the dogmatic order for the historical order. Only the former is able to arrive at a perfect state of our intelligence."[284]

Admittedly Comte weakens this thesis insofar as he concedes that the practice of scholars unavoidably amounts to a certain combination of dogmatic and historical organization of material, in which the former becomes increasingly more important. But the dogmatic principle cannot be applied too stringently. It calls for a logical-constructive revision of received knowledge, which can hardly be performed on its most recent stage. Moreover Comte sees that the dogmatic form of presentation exhibits a defect when it antiphilosophically and abruptly separates the finished results from the process through which they came about. According to Comte, however, his objection would be particularly burdensome only if it clearly spoke for the "historical order" (*ordre historique*). That, however, is not at all the case, for the chronological-historical study of a science deviates considerably from what Comte calls "the effective history of this science."[285] The latter encompasses more than is visible at first sight. Not only have the different scientific fields and sciences— which have been isolated from one another by the dogmatic order—developed simultaneously and under reciprocal influence, but the evolution of the human spirit is also closely bound up with the evolution of society. Therefore Comte stresses the necessity of studying the history of science in the general context of the history of humanity and its "social organization."[286] From this point of view, the documents which have been heretofore collected on the history of mathematics, astronomy, and medicine could count only as dead material.[287]

Comte is sharply critical of the supposedly historical form of presentation, which itself adheres to something hypothetical and abstract when it is strictly followed: the history of science remains a fact isolated from the social life process when in reality it forms its most important moment. Therefore Comte stresses the importance of conceiving a history of science that is both richer in content and sociologically grounded. In other words, whoever wants to become really familiar with a branch of research must appropriate its history. Nevertheless—and this connects Comte's reflections with those of Hegel and Marx—[288] in the future it will be essential to insist on the real difference between history (and historiography) of science, on the one hand, and its dogmatic investigation, on the other. Without such a distinction, that history to which Comte returns at the end of his *Cours de Philosophie positive*, not by chance, would not be understood at all.

Hegel and Marx took similar positions concerning the questions Comte discussed. Hegel, the speculative idealist, explicitly distinguished between the "path of the history of philosophy" and philosophy's "path in itself,"[289] which encompasses the concrete "totality of the idea."[290] Knowledge of the latter is served by the study of the history of philosophy (which Hegel had placed on more solid ground), but once formed it moves in its own medium and burns the bridges behind it. Just as stringently, Marx, the critic of political economy, keeps its history and system separate from one another. The "form of presentation" (*Darstellungsweise*) is based on the "form of inquiry" (*Forschungsweise*) but is "formally" distinct from it.[291] Beginning in the 1840s—according to recent literature—Marx divided his economic work into a specifically theoretical and a historical part.[292] From the outset, the latter recedes in importance in comparison with the systematic interest. In the *Poverty of Philosophy*, Marx countered Proudhon's unacceptable proposal, according to which one could "from the single logical formula of movement, of sequence, of time, explain the structure of society, in which all relations coexist simultaneously and support one another."[293] And in the *Introduction to the Critique of Political Economy* of 1857, which the structuralist authors regard as the Marxist *Discours de la méthode*, Marx wrote:

It would therefore be unfeasible and wrong to let the economic categories follow one another in the same sequence as that in which they were historically decisive. Their sequence is determined, rather, by their relation to one another in modern bourgeois society, which is precisely the opposite of that which seems to be their natural order or which corresponds to historical development. The point is not the historic position of the economic relations in the succession of different forms of society. Even less is it their sequence "in the idea" (Proudhon) (a muddy notion of historic movement). Rather, their order within modern bourgeois society.[294]

We should also recall that Marx, the historian of science, was too much of a dialectician to place blind faith in the historical course of the sciences. As political economy, in particular, demonstrates, their real starting point is reached only "through a multitude of contradictory moves. . . . Science, unlike other architects, builds not only castles in the air, but may construct separate habitable stories of the building before laying the foundation stone."[295]

To be sure, it is only with the help of the history of economic scholarship (as incorporating real history) that the "system of bourgeois economy"[296] that Marx investigated can be constructed. But the "presenting" (*darstellende*) logic of its structure does not in any sense coincide with the historical process that furnishes "mode of inquiry" with empirical materials. Not only the three volumes of *Theories of Surplus Value* but *Capital* as well testify to the intensity with which Marx studied historical sources of theory. The footnote apparatus, especially in volume 1 of *Capital*, contains a record of the residues of these studies.[297] Their results disappeared into Marx's system as the work of a tailor disappears into a finished coat.

Structuralist History of Science and Philosophy of History

It is the history of the natural sciences that most clearly shows how little the content of narrative history accords with that of its logically ordered, systematized content. When natural science attains a certain level, acquaintance with, even reflection on, the historical processes leading to it become ever more indispensable. The functioning of these processes in a given social sphere is immediately illuminating. Someone who has not studied the history of medicine, physics, or chemistry is not for that reason necessarily a bad doctor, physicist, or chemist. From this, structuralist history of science draws consequences which (irrespective of the remaining problems of continuity) are not at all incompatible with dialectic. The astounding extent to which these consequences are anticipated by Comte, Hegel, and Marx has already been outlined.

Serious differences arise, however, when the structuralists rather dogmatically transfer their insights into the history of science to history in general, and in so doing, as Lefebvre puts it, radically strip history of its drama. Unquestionably an antiphilosophical tendency expresses itself in this theoreticist turn of historical thinking, for the structure and subject matter of philosophy are not as independent from their own history—not to mention from world-historical processes—as are the structure and subject matter of the individual disciplines which are oriented to a mathematical concept of exactitude.

Conversely Comte, Hegel, and (in a sense that remains to be clarified) Marx as well remain philosophers of history (although with very different intentions). Of course, Comte placed the dogmatic structure of a science ahead of its temporal development. But he did not, on this account, decline to present his well-known "three-stage law" as the "law of the intellectual development of humanity."[298] For Comte, this law is the unity-producing subject of history, to which all theoretical and practical efforts refer.[299] His "encyclopedic law," which he assumed to correspond to an immutable hierarchy of the fundamental sciences—mathematics, astronomy, physics, chemistry, biology, and sociology—seeks to define their "dogmatic dependence" on one another as, simultaneously, a "historical sequence."[300] In so doing, Comte is eager to demonstrate an almost unnoticed continuity in the "history of the positive spirit," one which "moves from the simplest mathematical ideas to the highest social thinking."[301] Since the encyclopedic principle also serves to establish rational divisions within each basic science, the dogmatic stages and historical phases can approximate one another as closely as is required by the exactitude of comparison or the smooth transition (from one to the other).[302]

That Hegel, the speculative systematic thinker, was, in his manner of posing questions, no less important as a theorist of history (and historian)[303] and, as such, has stamped modern consciousness, are assertions that do not require further elaboration. What does need to be emphasized are those points which concern the relationship between theory and reality.

Contrary to superficial critique, the "standpoint of reason in world history" does not exhaust itself in a priori constructions which do violence to their material. Hegel stresses how little "the wish for rational insight, [and] for knowledge, not merely for a heap of facts,"[304] can be satisfied by fabricated concepts. Rather "in history thought is subordinated to the given and the existent."[305] He insists that we must respect the material before us and "must proceed historically—empirically."[306]

Nevertheless—and this is proper to a comprehending science which distinguishes the sensuous surface of facts from their true content—"reason presents a content which does not simply stand on the same line with that which has taken place in general."[307] Constructed and empirical history diverge from one another for epistemological reasons, not because philosophy abstracts from matters which contradict its program. In any case, Hegel admits that there is a great deal which can be incorporated into an immanent progression of reason, but only with great difficulty.

In world history, there are several great periods of development that have passed by apparently without continuing themselves:

On the contrary, after these periods the whole enormous gain in culture has been destroyed and unfortunately [people] had to go back to the beginning in order, with some support from those treasures saved from the ruins, with a renewed, immeasurable expenditure of energy and time . . . , to once again reach regions of culture that had been won long ago.[308]

Of course—this shows the questionable idealism of his method—Hegel immediately retreats from this objective insight by attributing it to inappropriate thinking. Continuing in the *Philosophie der Weltgeschichte*, Hegel writes that whoever adheres to a "formal principle of development in general"[309] possesses no certain criteria, and fails to see that

development . . . [is] not a mere emergence without harm and conflict, as is that of organic life. Rather it is hard, unwilling labor against itself . . . the bringing forth of a goal from particular content. We have established this goal from the beginning: it is spirit, and according to spirit's essence, the concept of freedom. This is . . . the leading principle of development, that through which it receives its meaning and significance.[310]

If, Hegel continues, the immanent goal of the world historical process is not adequately grasped, necessary progress or regression presents itself as an "external accident."[311]

Certainly Hegel succeeds in subjecting the historical process to a unified approach, one for which—in accordance with bourgeois economy—the accidental appearance is an objective expression of deeper laws. But this success comes at a high price. Hegel finds it necessary to write a theodicy, which in view of the "mass of concrete evils" from which history been composed until today, reconciles the thinking spirit with the negative."[312] The nameless suffering of individuals is of little concern to this conception: "particular goals are lost in the general goal."[313] The developing and already developed totality constitutes the substance of individuals. Hegel will not even afford consolation, which is in any case only "at home in the finite."[314] Hegel writes "Philosophy is . . . more. It reconciles and transfigures the real, which appears unjust, to the rational, shows it to be grounded in the idea itself and that with which reason should be content. For reason is a manifestation of God."[315] Thus Hegel explains the inner goal of history as the "final goal of the world."[316]

We know that Hegel's materialist students radically rejected the theological halo with which he surrounded the world historical process. At the same time, however, they adhered to his theory which claims that history is not a chaos of unrelated facts. Rather it presents supraindividual structures and tendencies that can be studied. The Hegelian philosophy of history, in Hegel's view, "is not preoccupied with individual, isolated situations, but with a general idea which passes through the whole."[317] In many places, Hegel expresses this idea (which materialists could start from) rather bluntly. The observing reason, he writes, "sees in emergence and disappearance the work which has resulted from the all-around labor of generations of humanity, a work that really is in the world which we belong to."[318]

Conscious individual activity, which remains, however, unconscious in relation to the total result, establishes the continuing interconnection of the process in the face of (indeed, by means of) all ruptures and leaps. For Hegel, its necessary stages are "only moments of a universal spirit, which through them elevates and makes itself into a self-comprehending totality in history."[319] Recent literature on the relationship of Marxism to Hegel, and in particular to the *Phenomenology of the Mind*, has pointed out in detail the remarkable extent to which the determinations of Hegel's "spirit" are borrowed from the sphere of social labor.[320] This is something that should be recalled in view of structuralist efforts to dismiss the idea of the world-constitutive role of historical praxis as being an ideological prejudice.

As for Marx and his students, they present considerably more difficult problems than do Comte or Hegel, problems arising from a curious double criticism. On the one hand, the critics of political economy can pass for "structuralists" (*avant la lettre*) of the day. The logical path of the analysis in *Capital* and the conception of a theory of history underlying it show, along with other sources, that they were averse to a naive-linear idea of history. I have already discussed the technical correctness of this view. On the other hand—Lukács pointed this out for the first time in *History and Class Consciousness*—Marxist theory, aiming at a "revolutionary practice" (*umwälzende Praxis*), breaks with the capitalist immediacy, which daily deludes individuals with a nature-like invariance of their life relationships. Lukács showed that even the historicism (which amounted to an extreme relativism) coming from the late bourgeois period was completely unable to treat adequately the "fundamental problem" which had been posed by the development of the capitalist world into a system: the problem of the "abolition of history." In Lukács's words, "The unexplained and inexplicable facticity of bourgeois existence as it is here and now acquires the patina of an eternal law of nature or a cultural value enduring for all time."[321] He added that the "unhistorical and antihistorical character of bourgeois thought" manifests itself most strikingly "when we consider the problem of the present as a historical problem."[322] Lukács's famous early work succeeded (irrespective of all the contemporary criticism of its "catastrophe theory" of history) in tolerating the contradiction between system and historical process. Consequently in *History and Class Consciousness* no unbridgeable chasm developed between diachronic and synchronic approaches. While the economic categories express real moments and levels of historical movement, their immanent connections constitute the "structural components of the present."[323]

Lukács, unlike the abstract "theory of the historical" in contemporary France which is oriented to the model of structuralist history of science, was preoccupied with the question (still contemporaneous) of structure-transforming praxis. In this question, living individuals and their destiny remain the order of the day. The fact that people are subsumed under oppressive structures does not mean that theory must resign itself merely to expressing this situation as precisely as possible. The "subject-lessness" (*Subjeklosigkeit*) of the whole is a theme of its critique, not an incontestable norm.

It is this claim which distinguishes Lukács from contemporary structuralists, toward whose problematic, in other respects, he comes remarkably close. Thus it is clear to him that the materialist dialectic of the course of history cannot be either ignored or deified. Its categories constitute "neither a purely logical sequence, nor are they organized merely in accordance with the facts of history." [324] Here Lukács has in mind Marx's insight (one which Althusser also repeatedly stresses) that the succession of and connection between categories are determined by "their mutual relation in modern bourgeois society and this is quite the reverse of what is in accordance with the sequence of historical development."[325] On the basis of Marx's insight, Lukács, of course, does not draw out any antihistorical consequences (that is, consequences directed against constitutive subjectivity). Rather he demonstrates that the Marxist idea of history does not repress but rather presupposes a positive conception of substantive history. It's essential to it

that the world which confronts man in theory and practice exhibits a kind of objectivity which—if properly thought out and understood—need never stick fast in an immediacy similar to that of forms found earlier on. This objectivity accordingly must be comprehensible as a constant factor mediating between past and future and it must be possible to demonstrate that it is everywhere the product of man and of the development of society.[326]

For Marx the methodologically established priority of the investigation of completed structures over research into their concrete development does not mean that the continuity of historical processes is irrelevant in the construction of theory.

One can agree with Godelier when he emphasizes that Marx,

in *Capital*, breaks away from every "empiricist, abbreviated writing of history."[327] The "historical-genetic analysis of a structure"[328] always presupposes a theory of the structure in question. It is only such analysis that uncovers the foundation which has led to the appearance of the inner elements of the structure and has placed these elements in relation to one another."[329] Nevertheless such a project contains within itself the danger, avoided by Marx, of becoming ideological. Methodological principles shift unnoticed into ontological ones. Vertical structures repress the horizontal structures. What is theoretically secondary for the present becomes null and void. Even Marx is a "structure"-thinker. But (and this brings us back to Lukács's reflections) he regards the petrified objectivity of the condition he investigates as something that is simultaneously subjective, that is, mediated by past labor. Lukács writes, "The historical knowledge of the proletariat begins with knowledge of the present, with the self-knowledge of its own social situation and with the elucidation of its necessity (i.e., its genesis)."[330] The latter, however, coincides with constitutive history. It is from this that the predominant structures, viewed methodologically, emerge.

This was an insight that was first directed at bourgeois scholarship. In the *Poverty of Philosophy*, Marx wrote, "The economists explain how production takes place in . . . given relations, but what they do not explain is how these relations themselves are produced, that is, the historical movement which gave them birth."[331] Since the official economics treats "the relations of bourgeois production, the division of labor, credit, money, etc., as fixed, immutable, eternal categories," Proudhon was understandably intent, Marx continues, on presenting "the act of formation, the genesis of these categories."[332] Marx then points out that Proudhon is totally unable to grasp the negative unity of the categorial (logical) and historical: soon he reduces real history to a mere "sequence of categories,"[333] and soon after that he believes that "real history according to the order in time"[334] immediately provides the canon for the sequence of ideas, categories, and principles. In Marx's view, Proudhon does not succeed in explaining the historical process with either approach. By contrast, Marx understands that the problematic of the relation of principles to history can be approached only through material studies. When, Marx writes, we pose the question

> why a particular principle was manifested in the eleventh or in the eighteenth century rather than in any other, we are necessarily forced to examine minutely what men were like in the eleventh century, what they were like in the eighteenth, what were their respective needs, their productive forces, their mode of production, the raw materials of their production—in short, what were the relations between man and man which resulted from all these conditions of existence. To get to the bottom of all these question—what is this but to draw up the real, profane history of men in every century and to present these men as both the authors and the actors of their own drama? But the moment you present men as the actors and authors of their own history, you arrive—by a detour—at the real starting point, because you have abandoned those eternal principles of which you spoke at the outset.[335]

The "real starting point" of science (Marx's political-economic works of the 1850s take up the term again) is not identical with its cognitive starting point. The dialectic in the work of the mature Marx can be characterized as a negative unity of structural and historical method. But it would be naive to believe that one can find comfort in this Hegelian formula. It requires further discussion, especially of the all-too-easily-overlooked "negativity" of such a unity. It is especially those schooled in the dialectic who will often be satisfied with unmediated (and therefore only "abstract") correctness and who explain that the point is not to neglect the aspects of development and history for the sake of the aspects of structure and analysis and vice-versa.[336] The stringent structuralists have performed a service in showing that such formulations do not settle the most delicate questions. The

task of Marxist theorists today consists in determinately negat-
ing the structuralist negation of history. This is something that
is easier said than done: The mere restoration of an eschatologi-
cal philosophy of history would remain unconvincing.

Summary

In view of the considerable difficulties that surface today in the
discussion of the theme history and structure, it may be useful,
once again, to recapitulate briefly the stages of the path tra-
versed in this book. We started out from the undisputed fact
(according to both adherents and opponents of structuralism)
that in *Capital* Marx used a method that was simultaneously
structural-analytic as well as historical-genetic. Of course viewpoints diverge widely over what such a "simulataneity" entails
and what sort of a dialectic it implies. If only in the form of
theses, I will follow up on the effort which I have undertaken in
order to contribute to a clarification of the question.

Marx characterizes the science founded by Engels and himself as "the conscious product of historical movement," which
does not at all mean that knowledge coincides with the historiography of its object or that it merely chronologically traces its
historical process. If Marx and Engels's theory was often understood in this way, the authors were not entirely blameless, for in
struggling against Hegel's timeless ontology, they accentuated
material history. They did so with good reason; in their view, the
point was to demonstrate both the coming-to-be (*Gewordenheit*)
and the transitoriness of the bourgeois relations of production.
However, in *Capital* this demonstration took place as "constructed" rather than "narrative" history. Once it comes into
existence, the capitalist system forms a stable structure extending over a long period of time. The investigator of its immanent
laws does not need to enter into their historical origin. More
precisely, he would be unable to do so as long as the essence of

capital is not conceptualized. Consequently one can speak of the "cognitive primacy of the logical over the historical" without in the least having to abandon the materialist basis.

The objective unity and difference between the history and the system of capitalism is reflected subjectively in the unity and difference between "mode of inquiry" (*Forschungsweise*) and "mode of presentation" (*Darstellungsweise*). Concerning the latter, I have investigated different aspects of the issue. I have referred to Marx's second Hegel reception and have tried to demonstrate what a constitutive as well as critical role Hegel's concept of system plays in the construction of Marx's economics. What is decisive is what Hegel, anticipating Marx, said concerning the complex connection of the "history of philosophy" to its "course in itself" (*Gang in sich*).

Against the background of these reflections on the Hegelian heritage of *Capital*, this book has investigated the Marx interpretations of the Althusser school and of Gramsci, interpretations which are instructive because they are in such glaring contradiction to one another. While Gramsci's "absolute historicism" or "humanism of history" identifies the theoretical process with the real course of history and with historiography (and practical politics), the Parisians consider Marxist doctrine as a "pure" theory averse to any substantive idea of history and to humanism. What is important in Gramsci are his general reflections on the scientific-theoretical status of Marx's theory and his more particular thoughts on the inner connection between historical materialism and the critique of political economy. Althusser's reassessment of Marx is useful insofar as he, after the cult of the "young Marx," energetically points to the philosophical content of *Capital* (which, to be sure, he interprets in a Spinozistic-rationalist manner). However, his supposedly anti-Hegelian insistence on the nonidentity of the structural and chronological succession of categories does not merit a great deal of attention. Hegel, as early as *The Phenomenology of the Mind*, not to mention his later works, was familiar with this problematic (one that returned in the Hegel student, Marx).

Nevertheless, with these arguments I have not disposed of the questions which have been raised and concepts which have been developed by the Althusser school. The rationalistic philosophy of the *nouvel esprit scientifique*, with its reduction of epistemology to constructed history of science (which without structuralist disadvantages already existed in Comte, Hegel, and Marx), is important in this connection because it constitutes an essential model of structural historical thinking in general. The last section indicates how it compares to a philosophy of history, which aims at "revolutionary praxis."

Notes

1. On this issue see my essay "Der strukturalistische Angriff auf die Geschichte," in *Beiträge zur marxistischen Erkenntnistheorie*, ed. Alfred Schmidt (Frankfurt am Main, 1969), pp. 194–265. The essay, which is directed against the Marx interpretation of the Althusser school, as well as against Lévi-Strauss, criticizes above all their tendency to eliminate the epistemological problem of subjectivity along with history (considered as human praxis). In the present work the issue of the textual justification for the structuralist theses concerning this problem will be examined in more detail.

2. Karl Marx and Friedrich Engels, *The German Ideology*, vol. 5 of *Karl Marx and Friedrich Engels: Collected Works* (New York, 1976), p. 28.

3. Ibid., p. 37.

4. Ibid., p. 42.

5. Ibid., p. 54.

6. Karl Marx, *The Poverty of Philosophy*, in *Marx and Engels: Collected Works*, vol. 6, p. 211.

7. Ibid., p. 177–178. These remarkable accounts of the relation between the representatives of a critical-proletarian literature to the world-historical process and to its driving forces in economic classes are based on the model of the anti-feudal struggle for emancipation waged by the West European bourgeoisie. In his 1947 polemical article directed against Karl Heinzen, "Moralising Criticism and Critical Morality," in *Marx and Engels: Collected Works*, vol. 6, pp. 312–340,

Marx wrote concerning that struggle, "The writer may very well serve a movement of history as its mouthpiece, but he cannot of course create it. . . . It was much more the case that the principles and theories put forward by the writers of the bourgeoisie during its struggle against feudalism were nothing but the theoretical expression of a series of real events; indeed one can see that the extent to which this expression was more or less utopian, dogmatic or doctrinaire corresponded exactly to the degree of advancement of the phase of real historical development" (p. 337). Indeed for Marx, the character of bourgeois emancipation as a model for proletarian emancipation refers not only to its method and direction but to its goal as well. The French Revolution up through the Paris Commune is crucial for his theory of revolution, yet Marx's theory pays insufficient attention to the politically decisive fact that even before 1789, the French bourgeoisie controlled the instruments of production, which, according to Marx, the proletariat was not supposed to appropriate until after its revolution.

8. Karl Marx, "Marx to J. B. Schweitzer, January 24, 1865," in *Marx/Engels: Selected Correspondence* (Moscow, 1975), p. 145. See also the oft-cited foreword to *A Contribution to the Critique of Political Economy* of 1859, in which he wrote that mankind sets itself only tasks that it can accomplish.

9. Karl Marx, *Capital*, vol. 1, trans. Ben Fowkes, introd. by Ernest Mandel (New York and London, 1976), preface to 1st ed., p. 92.

10. Ibid., preface to 2nd ed., p. 103.

11. Marx, *Grundrisse*, p. 278 (emphasis in original).

12. Ibid., p. 460.

13. Ibid., p. 461.

14. Ibid.

15. Ibid., p. 460.

16. The representatives of the Parisian Althusser school are in agreement with this view when they insist that the real object of Marx's *Capital* avoids the opposition (which dominated previous discussion) between abstract-theoretical economics and a concrete conception of history. Nicos Poulantzas writes that *Capital* is "neither an 'economic' nor a 'historical' work in the direct sense. Rather it is a work that permits the theoretical construction of the subject matter of history and economics, locating the concept of history and that of economy in the different modes of production . . . and circumscribing the economic as a sphere of theoretically specified structures for which a specific historical concept is developed, namely that of the process of transformation of forms." *Kritik der politischen Ökonomie heute. 100 Jahre 'Kapital,'* ed. Walter Euchner and Alfred Schmidt (Frankfurt am Main and Vienna, 1968), p. 68. Cf. on this issue, as well as on the structuralist interpretation of the mature Marx in general, the Althusserian

study "Marxism is not a historicism," in Louis Althusser and Etienne Balibar, *Reading Capital*, trans. Ben Brewster (London, 1970), pp. 119–144.

17. Karl Marx, *Grundrisse, Foundations of the Critique of Political Economy*, trans. Martin Nicolaus (Middlesex, England, and Baltimore, Md., 1973), p. 252.

18. Ibid.

19. Marx, *Capital*, 1:168.

20. Ludwig Feuerback, *Fragmente zur Charakteristik meines philosophischen Entwicklungsganges* (1843/1844), in *Sämtliche Werke*, ed. Wilhelm Bolin and Friedrich Jodl (Stuttgart, 1903–1911), vol. 2, p. 390 (emphasis in original).

21. Marx, *Capital*, 1:125.

22. Ibid., p. 714.

23. M. M. Rosenthal, *Die dialektische Methode der politischen Ökonomie von Karl Marx* (Berlin, 1969), p. 473. On the whole problematic of the "logical method" in *Capital*, see ibid., pp. 465–484. The question concerning categorial presentation (*kategorialer Darstellung*) is dealt with further by Helmut Reichelt in his important study, *Zur logischen Struktur des Kapitalbegriffs bei Marx* (Frankfurt am Main and Vienna, 1970). In particular see pp. 126–150.

24. Marx, *Capital*, 1:763.

25. Ibid., p. 715.

26. In this matter, as in others, Marxism owes a great deal to Hegelian philosophy, specifically, the much-discussed section "Independence and Dependence of Self-Consciousness: Lordship and Bondage" in *Phenomonology of the Mind*. It has rightly been interpreted, together with German Idealism in general, as being a speculative theory of the French Revolution, that is, as an attempt to conceptualize its world historical quintessence, a task that does not mean writing its history. As in *Capital*, the sequence of the *Phenomenology* does not leave the ground of history at any point. Yet it does not thereby present a through-going parallelism between reality and the spirit.

27. Frederick Engels, "Karl Marx. 'A Contribution to the Critique of Political Economy,'" pp. 218–227 in Marx, *Contribution to the Critique of Political Economy*, p. 220.

28. Ibid., p. 224.

29. Ibid., p. 222.

30. Ibid., p. 224.

31. Ibid.

32. Ibid.

33. Ibid., p. 225.

34. Ibid.

35. Marx, *Capital*, p. 169 (emphasis in original).

36. Rosenthal, *Die dialektische Methode*, p. 464.

37. Engels, "Karl Marx," p. 225. On the epistemological aspect of this problematic, see my essay "Über Geschichte und Geschichtsschreibung in der materialistischen Dialektik," in *Folgen einer Theorie. Essays uber 'Das Kapital' von Karl Marx* (Frankfurt am Main, 1967), pp. 103–129.

38. Rosenthal, *Die dialektische Methode*, p. 469.

39. Karl Marx, "Marx to Kugelmann, Letter of June 27, 1870," in *Marx/Engels: Selected Correspondence*, pp. 225–226 (emphasis in original).

40. Marx, *Grundrisse*, introduction, p. 107.

41. Marx, *Capital*, 1:102.

42. G. W. F. Hegel, *The Philosophy of Nature*, trans. M. J. Petry (New York and London, 1970), pp. 201–202. On the distinction between the "mode of inquiry" and the "mode of presentation" in Marx, see my essay, "Zum Erkenntnisbegriff der Kritik der politischen Ökonomie," in *Kritik der politischen Ökonomie heute*, pp. 34–38.

43. Ibid., p. 202.

44. Ibid.

45. Ibid., p. 203. I have consciously drawn on Hegel's *Philosophy of Nature*, a work with which Marx was familiar. For all its abstruseness, it is of great interest today, especially with regard to its methodological project. Hegel's explanation of the qualitative difference between analytic and dialectical reason in physics serves the purpose of the present study insofar as modern sociology has been oriented largely on the model of the natural sciences since Saint Simon's "physicism" (*Physizismus*).

46. Marx, *Grundrisse*, introduction, p. 101.

47. Karl Marx, "Marx an Engels, Brief vom 9.12.1861," in *Marx/Engels Werke* (Berlin, 1964), vol. 30, p. 207.

48. Marx, *Grundrisse*, introduction, p. 99.

49. Karl Marx, *Theories of Surplus Value: Part III* (Moscow, 1971), p. 500.

50. Ibid.

51. Marx, *Grundrisse*, introduction, p. 100.

52. Ibid.

53. Cf. ibid.

54. Ibid.

55. Herbert Marcuse, *Reason and Revolution* (Boston, 1960), pp. 314–320.

56. Marx, *Grundrisse*, introduction, p. 99.

57. Ibid., p. 101.

58. Ibid.

59. Ibid.

60. G. W. F. Hegel, *Lectures on the History of Philosophy*, vol. 3, trans. E. S. Haldane and Frances H. Simon (New York and London, 1896; reprint ed., 1974), pp. 176–177.

61. Ibid., p. 176.

62. Ibid.

63. Ibid.

64. Ibid.

65. Ibid.

66. Marx, *Capital*, 1:167–168.

67. On this point see my essay, "Die strukturalistische Angriff auf die Geschichte," which criticizes the unmediated "objectivism" of structuralist authors.

68. Marx, *Grundrisse*, p. 239.

69. Ibid., p. 252.

70. Ibid., p. 459 (emphasis in original).

115

History and Structure

71. Ibid., p. 460.

72. Ibid.

73. Of course already in *The German Ideology*, in contrast to the mere collection and ordering of historical materials, the qualitatively higher concept of the "presentation . . . of . . . the thing in its totality" emerges, although in undeveloped form. Cf. on this issue my "Über Geschichte und Geschichtsschreibung in der materialistischen Dialektik," p. 122.

74. Karl Marx, "Marx to Lassalle, Letter of February 22, 1858," in *Marx/Engels: Selected Correspondence*, pp. 96–97.

75. Marx, *Grundrisse*, p. 253.

76. Rosenthal, *Die dialektische Methode*, p. 472.

77. Marx, *Capital*, 1:714.

78. Rosenthal, *Die dialektische Methode*, p. 472.

79. Marx, *Grundrisse*, p. 253.

80. Marx, *Capital*, 1:247.

81. Ibid., p. 90.

82. V. I. Lenin, *Philosophical Notebooks*, vol. 38 of *Collected Works* (Moscow, 1961), pp. 178–179 (emphasis in original).

83. Ibid., p. 320 (emphasis in original). Cf. also p. 30, where Lenin emphasizes that the "idea of the social relations of production" constitutes the "basic idea" of the Marxian "system."

84. Ibid., p. 320 (emphasis in original).

85. Cf. on this point Engels, *Karl Marx: A Contribution*, p. 225–226.

86. Marx, *Capital*, 1:125.

87. Ibid., p. 176.

88. G. W. F. Hegel, *Science of Logic*, trans. A. V. Miller (New York and London, 1969), p. 71. As a dialectical thinker, Marx thought a great deal about the simultaneously unmediated and mediated character of the beginnings of theory. In doing so he was clearly oriented to what Hegel's famous segment "With What Must the Science Begin?" (cf. ibid., pp. 67–78) had to say on the subject. Deeply grounded in the history of dogma, Marx knows very well that his starting point in the analysis of commodities (labor as concrete and abstract activity that brings

forth use value and exchange value) in no sense originates only from his intentional choice or from the composition (and genesis) of the object of his research. Rather it stems as well from the general path of the science of political economy. The development of the latter proceeds in such a manner that scholars (Marx mentions the Physiocrats in reference to the question of value) frequently treat problems in a more complicated form before they are in a position to secure the elementary initial evaluations necessary for more advanced work. In general, as Marx demonstrates, "the historical path" of the sciences "leads only through a multitude of contradictory moves to their real point of origin. . . . As distinguished from other master-builders, science builds not only castles in the air, but may construct separate habitable stories of the building before laying the foundation stone." Engels, *Karl Marx: A Contribution*, p. 57.

89. Ibid., p. 70.

90. Ibid (emphasis in original).

91. Ibid., pp. 70–71.

92. Marx, *Grundrisse*, introduction, p. 100.

93. Ibid., p. 101.

94. Marx, *Capital*, 1:90.

95. Ibid., p. 101.

96. Marx, *Grundrisse*, introduction, p. 101.

97. Ibid., p. 101–102.

98. Hegel, *Science of Logic*, p. 72.

99. Ibid., p. 841.

100. Marx, *Grundrisse*, p. 460.

101. Ibid.

102. Ibid., p. 461.

103. Marx, *Grundrisse*, introduction, p. 105.

104. Marx, *Grundrisse*, p. 461.

105. Marx, *Grundrisse*, introduction, p. 105.

106. Ibid.

107. Ibid.

108. Ibid., p. 106.

109. Karl Marx, *Grundrisse der Kritik der Politischen Ökonomie* (Berlin, 1953), p. 945.

110. Ibid.

111. Ibid (emphasis in original).

112. Ibid., p. 922. [The material cited in notes 109–112 does not appear in the English translation. All subsequent references the Marx's *Grundrisse* refer to the Nicolaus translation.]

113. Marx, *Grundrisse*, p. 885.

114. Ibid.

115. Ibid., p. 649.

116. Ibid., pp. 649–650.

117. Ibid.

118. Ibid., p. 650.

119. Ibid.

120. Ibid.

121. Ibid., p. 651.

122. Ibid. On the objective dialectic of chance and necessity (which is important for Marx's theory in general), also see *Capital*, 1:429. In addition see G. W. F. Hegel, *Philosophy of Right*, trans. T. M. Knox (Oxford, 1965), sec. 189, in which Hegel writes that the task of political economy is to work "upon the endless mass of details which confront it at the outset and extracting therefrom the simple principles of the thing, the Understanding effective in the thing and directing it" (p. 127).

123. Ibid., p. 650.

124. Ibid. (emphasis in original).

125. Ibid. (emphasis in original).

126. Ibid.

127. Ibid., p. 651.

128. Ibid., p. 463. This idea again makes clear the limits of the structuralist Marx interpretation as it is put forward by the Althusserian school in Paris. For example, Nicos Poulantzas differentiates two disciplines within the unity of Marxism on the basis of their different objects: dialectical and historical materialism. The latter—"the science of history"—defines its object as "the constitution of the concept of history," the former—"Marxist philosophy"—is understood by Poulantzas in a gnoseological sense. It is concerned with "the production of knowledge, that is the structure and functioning of the process of thought," which amounts to a "theory of the history of scientific production." Nicos Poulantzas, *Political Power and Social Classes*, trans. Timothy O'Hagen (London, 1975), p. 11. Poulantzas is certainly right when he emphasizes how mistaken it is to reduce materialist epistemology to the materialist conception of history. He rejects the "historicist interpretations" (whereby he mentions the young Lukács and Korsch) in which Marxism is "a historical anthropology, of which history is an originating and basic category rather than a concept to be constructed. Reflection on structures, 'gaining consciousness of their meaning,' is a function of the structures themselves, which are interiorized in a process of mediation" (ibid.). The question arises whether Poulantzas (who with his teacher, Althusser, wishes to obliterate all Hegelian traces in Marxism) does not, in this manner, fall into the contrasting mistake which he himself designated as "positivist-empiricist interpretations." Such interpretations narrow historical materialism to the barren skeleton of a universally valid "law" (or "model") which from time to time is only to be "concretized" with historical examples (ibid.). How else should one interpret Poulantzas's thesis that historical materialism deals primarily with the "concept" of history? Doesn't this concept presuppose the study of the content of the course of history, in other words, narrative history? (This is something which Poulantzas will probably admit, if only in abstracto.) Of course in Marx's *Capital* there is "constructed" history but also, in the materialist sense, creative "praxis." It is hard to understand why a dialectical theory is supposed to bring both concepts into unmediated (even unmediatable) opposition as is the case with Poulantzas.

129. Marx, *Capital*, 1:273.

130. Ibid., p. 273.

131. Ibid., p. 273–274 (emphasis in original). Cf. also Marx, *Grundrisse der Kritik der Politischen Ökonomie*, p. 945.

132. Marx, *Grundrisse*, p. 461.

133. Engels, *Karl Marx: A Contribution*, p. 225.

134. Hegel, *Science of Logic*, p. 611.

135. In view of the structuralist interpretation (see note 128) it should be emphatically stressed that even *Capital* (in spite of and as a consequence of its

method, which is focused on objectivity) contains the idea, supporting the whole of Marxist analysis, that what matters is to make transparent the developed and developing nature of existing structures, to mediate them with practical subjectivity. The enduring contribution of *History and Class Consciousness* is to have pointed this out energetically. Thus in his essay, "Reification and the Consciousness of the Proletariat" (which is especially instructive for the future construction of a Marxist historical method), Lukács shows the difficulties which Hegel fell into because the relationship between absolute spirit and history ("world spirit") remains unexplained. By suspending real history, Hegel's philosophy comes to a timeless conceptual kind of genesis, one taken over from, yet at the same time denying, reality, a genesis which moves from logic through nature to spirit: "But as the historicity of all categories and their movements intrudes decisively into the dialectical method and as dialectical genesis and history necessarily belong together objectively . . . this process which had been designed to be suprahistorical, inevitably exhibits a historical structure at every point." George Lukács, *History and Class Consciousness*, trans. Rodney Livingstone (Cambridge, Mass., 1971), pp. 147–48. Thereby Hegel's method takes on an "abstract-contemplative" character, which, on the one hand, causes it to "falsify and do violence to" history. On the other hand, "history will gain its revenge and violate the method which has failed to integrate it, tearing it to pieces." Hence (here Lukács recalls Marx's critique of Hegel) the "demiurgic role of the 'spirit'" will manifest itself as pure "conceptual mythology" (ibid). Just as sharply, Lukács attacks the tendency of modern theorists of history (of Rickert's type) to remain immersed in the crude immediacy of the factual, tied, of course, to "values" which allow only a "selection" from their abundance, leave facticity itself unchanged, and confront it only accidentally and externally (ibid., p. 151). What is thereby achieved is merely "a formal typology of the manifestations of history and society using historical facts as illustrations" (ibid., p. 154, emphasis in original). On the other hand, what Lukács has in mind is a binding self-interpretation of historically moved being— that is, a theory in which the objective reality of events is not described from a neutral, external standpoint but rather is one in which the world-historical content of these events becomes transparent. Therefore he emphasizes that it was only with Marxism that the dialectic actually could become a "method of history" by devolving on the proletariat, a class "which was able to discover within itself on the basis of its life-experience . . . the subject of action, the 'we' of genesis" (ibid., p. 149). "The historical knowledge of the proletariat," on the basis of Marx's *Capital*, "begins with knowledge of the present, with the self-knowledge of its own social situation and with the elucidation of its necessity (i.e., its genesis)" (ibid., p. 159).

136. Cf. Althusser's essay "Marxism and Humanism," in *For Marx* (New York, 1970), pp. 219–247. Also see Nicos Poulantzas's lecture "Theorie und Geschichte. Kurze Bemerkungen über den Gegenstand des 'Kapitals,'" delivered at the Frankfurt Colloquium in September 1967 and reprinted in *Kritik der politischen Ökonomie heute*, pp. 58–69. For a critique of these Althusserian positions see also Wolf Lepennies/Helmut Nolte, *Kritik der Anthropologie* (Munich, 1971), p. 68.

137. Marx, *Capital*, 1:932. On the implicit humanism of Marx's theoretical ef-

forts, see also my study, *Die "Zeitschrift fur Sozialforschung," Geschichte und Gegenwärtige Bedeutung* (Munich, 1970), pp. 33–38.

138. Marx, *Contribution to the Critique*, p. 152.

139. Hegel, *Science of Logic*, p. 801. Hence Marx in the "Introduction to the Critique of Political Economy" (the introduction to the *Grundrisse*) of 1857 takes up Hegel's theory almost word for word. The concrete is a "manifold connection" of abstract determinations of thought (cf. *Science of Logic*, p. 801.)

140. Ibid.

141. Ibid. Cf. also ibid., p. 588, where Hegel sets forth with the desired sharpness the difference between a reasoned cognition and historical thinking (in the broadest sense). It is not altogether prudent for the structuralists to direct their attack at a "Hegelian" interpretation of Marx in particular, for it is *The Science of Logic* [*Greater Logic*], which, in many places, supports their own critique of historicism.

142. Lukács, *History and Class Consciousness*, p. 159.

143. Althusser, *For Marx*, p. 193. Here Althusser orients himself to Marx's "Introduction" of 1857.

144. Marx, *Grundrisse*, introduction, p. 85.

145. Althusser, *For Marx*, p. 195.

146. Ibid., pp. 195–96.

147. Ibid., p. 199.

148. This becomes particularly clear in Althusser's treatment of the doctrine of contradiction. His most important authority in *For Marx* is Mao Tse-tung, whose rather formalistic and ontologically naive conception of the dialectic he appears to share.

149. Raymond Aron, *Die heiligen Familien des Marxismus* (Hamburg, 1970), p. 209. See also p. 208 where Aron (who, from an opposing political stance, arrives at important insights, especially in relation to the economics and history of Marxism) confronts Althusser's "attempt at timeless historical knowledge" with Lévi-Strauss's "wild thinking."

150. Marx, *Grundrisse*, introduction, p. 101.

151. Ibid., p. 86.

152. Ibid., p. 101.

153. Ibid.

154. Ibid.

155. Ibid., p. 102.

156. Ibid.

157. Ibid.

158. Ibid. Cf. also p. 103. On the special form of the unity of the historical and the logical, see also the essay by Gunther Kohlmey, "Zum Erkenntnis in der marxistischen politischen Okonomie," in *Probleme der politischen Ökonomie* (Berlin, 1959), pp. 81–85.

159. Marx, *Capital*, vol. 1, postface to the 2nd ed., p. 102.

160. Cf. Althusser/Balibar, *Reading Capital* (New York, 1970), p. 119.

161. Above all Croce and Gentile, whose thought he nevertheless criticized as limited to the speculative-theological realm.

162. Cf. Jacques Texier, *Gramsci et la philosophie du marxisme* (Paris, 1966), especially pp. 13–20. Adorno's Marx interpretation also contains this historical element. On Gramsci's thought as a whole, cf. the knowledgeable and critical study by Christian Riechers, *Antonio Gramsci: Marxismus in Italien* (Frankfurt am Main, 1970).

163. Antonio Gramsci, *Philosophie der Praxis*, ed. and trans. Christian Riechers (Frankfurt am Main, 1967) p. 253; cf. also p. 197.

164. Ibid., p. 253.

165. *Antonio Gramsci: Selections from the Prison Notebooks*, ed. and trans. Quinton Hoare and Geoffrey Novell Smith (New York, 1971), p. 428.

166. Ibid.

167. Karl Marx, *Capital* (Moscow, 1962), vol. 3, p. 141. Cf. ibid., where Marx writes that he has not presented "the real movement of competition" but "only the inner organization of the capitalist mode of production, so to speak, in its ideal average." Along similar lines, Lenin criticized Struve because he confused "the abstract theory of realization . . . with concrete historical conditions governing the realization of the capitalist product in some one country and some one epoch." "Once More on the Theory of Realization," in *Collected Works*, 4:75. Lenin, like Marx, emphasized that the "law of capitalism . . . depicts only the ideal of capitalism and not its reality" (ibid., p. 86). It is implemented "only by not being implemented" (ibid., p. 77). From all this it certainly does not follow that Max Weber's all-too-nominalist interpretation is right. According to Weber,

"All specifically Marxian laws and development constructs . . . are ideal types."
Weber underscores the "eminent, indeed unique, *heuristic* significance of these
ideal types when they are used for the *assessment* of reality" and at the same time
warns of "their perniciousness as soon as they are thought of as empirically valid
or as real (i.e., truly metaphysical) 'effective forces,' 'tendencies,' etc." Max Weber,
The Methodology of the Social Sciences, trans. and ed. Edward A. Shils and Henry
A. Finch (New York, 1949), p. 103 (emphasis in original). Of course Weber was
right when, in this context, he pointed out how unserious it is to turn historical
knowledge into "a servant of theory instead of the other way around. It is a great
temptation for the theorist to regard this relationship either as the normal one
or, far worse, to mix theory with history and indeed to confuse them with each
other" (ibid., emphasis in original). That something like that has not uncom-
monly appeared in the Marxist tradition is obvious. However to admit this does
not dispose of the legitimate claim of Marxist theory: to get hold of objective-
real circumstances by means of its constructions. In contrast to Weber's ideal
types, Marxist categories are *entia rationis cum fundamento in re*. The class-political
accent of the Weberian conception (he expresses it in the then-current objection
that Marx advocated a "materialistic metaphysic") lies in its subjectivism which
reduces Marxist structural laws to the level of heuristic fictions with whose help
the irrational reality (consisting of an enormous sum of singular facts) will be
ordered.

168. Hegel, *Science of Logic*, pp. 503–504 (emphasis in original).

169. Hegel's theory of the law as the stable image of appearances impressed
Lenin, whose conspectus on the *Science of Logic* notes: "This is a remarkably
materialistic and remarkably appropriate (with the word 'ruhige') determination.
Law takes the quiescent—and therefore law, every law, is narrow, incomplete,
approximate." V. I. Lenin, *Lenin: Collected Works*, 38:151. The idea that appearances are richer than law (ibid., p. 152) comes from Hegel himself but contains
an aspect which remained in the background in Hegel's theory but developed
further in dialectical materialism. While Hegel rejected as an "abstract" precau-
tion the general thesis according to which all human stages of knowledge have a
merely approximate significance owing to their historical and transitory nature
and called for the "exertion of the concept," which is to be continuously performed anew, Marxist materialism (in this respect more strongly oriented to the
actual course of scientific research) from the outset is guided by the former thesis
in the construction of its concepts. On this question cf. the essay (which picks up
the threads of Lenin's Hegel interpretation) by Wilhelm Raimund Beyer, "Hegel's 'Law,'" in *Der Gesetzesbegriff in der Philosophie und den Einzelwissenschaften*, ed.
Günter Kröber (Berlin, 1968), p. 47. Beyer stresses the "correctibility," "com-
pleteability," and "controllability" of the materialistically conceived concept of
law.

170. Marx, *Capital*, 1:411.

171. Ibid., p. 492. In a review of *Capital*, Engels rightly speaks of the "analytic
principles of the recent history of industry" which Marx presented, in Marx/
Engels, *Werke*, Band 16 (Berlin, 1968), p. 229.

172. *Gramsci: Selections*, pp. 427–428. On this question in general, cf. Gramsci's comment on Bukharin's Marxism, "Critical Notes on an Attempt at Popular Sociology," in ibid., pp. 419–472.

173. Nikolai Bukharin, *Historical Materialism* (Ann Arbor, 1969), p. 14.

174. Ibid., p. 15.

175. Here it should be recalled that Marx and Engels define the relation between theory and theoretical practice of materialist historical writing differently. Both reciprocally correct one another from case to case. In *The German Ideology* they write; "When the reality is described, a self-sufficient philosophy [*die selbständige Philosophie*] loses its medium of existence. At best, its place can only be taken by a summing up of the most general results, abstractions which are derived from the observation of the historical development of men. Those abstractions in themselves, divorced from real history, have no value whatsoever. They can only serve to facilitate the arrangement of historical material, to indicate the sequence of its separate strata. But they by no means afford a recipe or schema, as does philosophy, for neatly trimming the epochs of history. On the contrary, the difficulties begin only when one sets about the examination and arrangement of the material—whether of a past epoch or of the present—and its actual presentation. The removal of these difficulties is governed by promises which certainly cannot be stated here but which only the study of the actual life process and the activity of the individuals of each epoch will make evident." Marx and Engels, *The German Ideology*, p. 37.

176. *Gramsci: Selections*, p. 434. This factually and textually unsupportable departmentalization has continued in Soviet Marxist textbooks up to the present. Of course, today an effort is made to formulate it less crudely.

177. Ibid., p. 436; cf. also on this "identity of history and philosophy," Gramsci, *Philosophie der Praxis*, p. 268.

178. Ibid., p. 431.

179. On the critique of this historiographical effort by Croce, cf. "Notes on Italian History," p. 118.

180. Gramsci, *Philosophie der Praxis*, pp. 268–269. Unfortunately we must forgo a closer examination of Gramsci's theory of ideology. Next to the pejorative concept of ideology going back to Marx (ideology as a passive "reflex," "necessary appearance" of material existence; cf. ibid., p. 271), Gramsci grasps a "positive" concept which, according to him, results from the "identity of philosophy and politics" and which does not allow ideologies—Gramsci (along with Croce) characterizes them as "instruments of political action"—to be separated from philosophy. In the final analysis, they are identical. "Ideologies," Gramsci writes, "will be the 'true' philosophy because they set forth philosophical 'popularizations' which induce the masses to concrete action toward the transformation of reality. In this way, they become the mass aspect of every philosophical concep-

tion which, among philosophers, assumes the character of an abstract universality beyond space and time, the special character of its literary and unhistorical origins" (ibid., p. 268). For all that, Gramsci is aware of the danger inherent in the identification of philosophy and ideology (cf. ibid., p. 269).

181. Ibid., p. 253.

182. Ibid., p. 270.

183. Ibid.

184. Ibid.

185. Ibid., p. 271.

186. Ibid., p. 272; cf. also p. 271.

187. Ibid., p. 273.

188. Ibid., p. 271.

189. Ibid., p. 253.

190. *Gramsci: Selections*, p. 399.

191. Ibid., p. 405. The idea of the "disunity" of human essence connects Gramsci with the beginning of critical theory. On this cf. Max Horkheimer, "Bemerkungen zur philosophischen Anthropologie," in *Zeitschrift für Sozialforschung* (IV, 1935), 1:1–25 (vol. 4 of the 1970 reprint of the *Zeitschrift* by Kösel).

192. On this cf. as well Riechers, *Gramsci: Marxismus in Italien*, p. 142. Riechers uncovers remarkable parallels between Gramsci and Bagdonov.

193. On this cf. the collection of essays by Croce, *Il concetto della storia*, ed. with introd. Alfredo Parente (Bari, 1967), p. 9.

194. Most of Gramsci's works were written in prison, in bad health and without scholarly apparatus. These conditions account for many defects. In terms of substance (as is demonstrated by Riechers's sober, myth-destroying book, especially, pp. 10–36) these shortcomings can be traced back to the fact that in his formative years Gramsci was influenced not only by Croce's Hegelianism but just as much by the appropriation of "residues of monistic consciousness from Labriola's philosophical past" (cf. ibid., pp. 16, 18) in bourgeois-academic authors such as Gentile and Mondolfo, who interpreted Marxism in a subjectivist-idealist manner. The term *philosophy of praxis* comes from Cieszkowskis, *Prolegomena zur Historiosophie* (Berlin, 1838), and was introduced into the Italian discussion around the turn of the century by Labriola.

195. Gramsci, *Philosophie der Praxis*, p. 192.

196. Ibid., pp. 192–93.

197. V. I. Lenin, "The Three Sources and Three Component Parts of Marxism," in *Lenin: Selected Works in Three Volumes* (New York, 1967), p. 41 (emphasis in original).

198. *Gramsci: Selections*, p. 399.

199. Ibid., p. 400.

200. Ibid.

201. Ibid.

202. Ibid., p. 401.

203. Marx and Engels, *The German Ideology*, p. 51 (emphasis in original).

204. *Gramsci: Selections*, p. 401.

205. Ibid.

206. Ibid.

207. Ibid. Gramsci (of course in a tentative and programmatic way) anticipated results of modern research. See the important book by the Czech philosopher, Jindrich Zeleny, *Die Wissenschaftslogik bei Marx und "Das Kapital"* (Berlin, 1968), especially chapters 1–2, in which Zeleny interprets the Marx-Ricardo connection in terms of a critique of one-sided quantitativism.

208. *Gramsci: Selections*, p. 404.

209. Ibid., p. 405.

210. At the same time, it is clear that without the concept of law taken from physics since Galileo and Newton, neither Saint-Simon's "social physics" nor Marx's manner of speaking of social "laws of motion" would have been conceivable. On this difficult problem, see my contribution in *Kritik der politischen Ökonomie heute*.

211. *Gramsci: Selections*, p. 410. For Gramsci's estimation of Ricardo's role in the emergence of Marxist theory, see ibid., p. 412.

212. Ibid., pp. 410–411.

213. Ibid., p. 411.

214. Ibid., p. 403; cf. also p. 395.

215. Cf. such a political work as Marx's *Critique of the Gotha Program*, written in 1875, when Marx had long ago left specifically philosophical controversies behind. At the same time, however, it contains an idea that is indispensable for materialist epistemology: that human labor (understood as "form giving," sensuous-concrete activity) always refers to an already-"formed," existing natural substratum independent from it. See Karl Marx, "Critique of the Gotha Program," in *Karl Marx and Frederick Engels: Selected Works* (New York, 1968), p. 319. Taking as my point of departure the idea that one must not assume that Marx is most philosophical only when he uses the language of academic philosophy, I have attempted in my book *The Concept of Nature in Marx*, trans. Ben Fowkes (London, 1971), to distill the philosophically important content of Marx's political-economic works. In *Reading Capital*, Althusser rightly emphasizes the necessity of unfolding Marxist philosophy on the basis of Marx's *Capital*. However, that cannot mean that one can either overlook the genetic (and also textual) connection between Marx's mature work and his early writings or abstractly deny Hegel's influence on the mature Marx, as Althusser does in his interpretation.

216. It is obvious that all of this is not a matter of merely literary or didactic questions. Lenin devoted some attention to the intimate and inseparable relationship of philosophy to political economy in Marx. Cf. his essay "Socialism Demolished Again," *Collected Works* (Moscow, 1964), vol. 20, p. 193, in which he demonstrates (while polemicizing against Struve) that the "unity" of Marx's materialist world view is grounded in the unity of philosophy and political economy.

217. Jurgen Ritsert and Egon Becker, *Grundzüge sozialwissenschaftlichstatistischer Argumentation* (Oplanden, West Germany, 1971), p. 30. Cf. also pp. 12, 31 of this important book.

218. Theodor Adorno, *Negative Dialectics*, trans. E. B. Ashton (New York, 1973), p. 355–356.

219. Ibid., p. 355.

220. In many ways, the idea of pure historicity connects Gramsci to Heidegger's *Being and Time*, to Marcuse's ontological beginnings, but especially to Lukács's early essays. On this see my contribution to the discussion with Furio Cerutti, Dtelev Claussen, Hans-Jurgen Krahl, and Oskar Negt, in *Geschichte und Klassenbewusstein heute* (Frankfurt am Main, 1971), pp. 8–16.

221. The original version (Paris, 1965) also contains contributions by Roger Establet, Jacques Ranciere, and Pierre Macherey. In order to gain a complete overview, one must refer to them. Also important is Maurice Godelier, *Rationality and Irrationality in Economics* (London, 1972).

222. Althusser/Balibar *Reading Capital*, p. 7.

223. See Rolf Dlubek and Hannes Skambrak, *"Das Kapital" von Karl Marx in der deutschen Arbeiterbewegung: 1867–78* (Berlin, 1967) on the history of the political

and literary impact of *Capital*. It contains an instructive historical outline, augmented by a collection of documents.

224. Karl Kautsky, *The Economic Doctrines of Karl Marx* (New York, 1936).

225. Franz Mehring, *Über historischen Materialismus* (Berlin, 1952), p. 37.

226. Ibid., p. 36.

227. On the specifically French ideological-historical presuppositions of the Marx interpretation coming from Althusser and his students, cf. my essay "Der strukturalistische Angriff auf die Geschichte."

228. On this theoretical devaluation of "humanism" and "historicism," see Urs Jaeggi's lucid analysis in his book *Ordnung und Chaos: Der Strukturalismus als Methode und Mode* (Frankfurt am Main, 1968), p. 154.

229. See Schmidt, "Der Strukturalistische Angriff auf die Geschichte," pp. 202–204.

230. V. I. Lenin, *Imperialism: The Highest Stage of Capitalism* in *Collected Works*, 22:200 (emphasis added).

231. V. I. Lenin, "An Uncritical Criticism," *Collected Works* (Moscow, 1964), vol. 3, p. 617.

232. V. I. Lenin, "Once More on the Theory of Realisation," *Collected Works*, 4:92.

233. Ibid., p. 89.

234. In recent years, a number of important books on Marxist economics have appeared which investigate the question of its relationship to history. In addition to those already mentioned are the essay collection edited by Georg Mende and Erhard Lange, *Die aktuelle philosophische Bedeutung des "Kapital" von Karl Marx* (Berlin, 1968) and the revised edition of Otto Morf's 1951 work, *Geschichte und Dialektik in der politischen Ökonomie: Zum Verhältnis von Wirtschaftstheorie und Wirtschaftsgeschichte bei Karl Marx* (Frankfurt am Main/Vienna, 1970).

235. Cf. on this the instructive and bibliographically helpful study by Paul Ginestier, *La Pensée de Bachelard* (Paris, 1968), pp. 25–123.

236. Cf. ibid., p. 26. Of course Comte himself is one of the founders of structuralist historical thinking. On this cf. Michel Pécheux and Michel Fichant's Althusserian-inspired book, *Sur l'histoire des sciences* (Paris, 1969).

237. Gaston Bachelard, *La formation de l'esprit scientifique: contribution à une psychanalyse de la connaissance objective* (Paris, 1938), p. 123.

238. Gaston Bachelard, *La valeur inductive de la relativité* (Paris, 1929), p. 6.

239. Gaston Bachelard, *Étude sur l'évolution d'un problême de physique: la propagadation thermique dans les solides* (Paris, 1928), p. 7.

240. As Georges Canguilhem has shown in his book, *La formation du concept de réflexe aux XVII et XVIII siècles* (Paris, 1955), the history of the theory of the reflex arc shows the exact conditions under which the word *reflex* became a scientifically applicable concept. Upon investigation it becomes surprisingly clear that this concept springs from a "vitalist" rather than "mechanistic" problematic. On Canguilhem cf. see André Noiray, *La philosophie de Hegel a Foucault, du marxisme à la phénoménologie* (Paris, 1969), p. 56. On modern French epistemology in general, see the excellent article *L'épistémologie* by François Guéry, ibid., p. 120–49.

241. See Noiray, *La philosophie de Hegel à Foucault.*

242. On this concept see Guéry, *L'épistémologie.*

243. Cf. ibid., p. 130.

244. Ibid.

245. Nevertheless, as Bachelard explains in terms of the concept of "specific heat" (which came from Black's distinction between quantities of heat and temperature in 1760), contemporary thought has an interest in that long past whose concepts have been incorporated into science.

246. Noiray, ed., *La philosophie*, p. 119.

247. Ibid., p. 221.

248. Concerning the connection between genetic and historical theory, I am following Guéry, *L'épistémologie.*

249. On Bachelard's concept of the dialectic, see Ginestier, *La pensée de Bachelard*, pp. 39–46.

250. Bachelard, *Essai sur la connaissance approchée* (Paris, 1928), p. 300.

251. Gaston Bachelard, *The Philosophy of No; A Philosophy of the New Scientific Mind*, trans. G. C. Waterston (New York, 1968), pp. 122–123.

252. Ginestier, *La pensée de Bachelard*, p. 38. Cf. also p 43.

253. Ibid., p. 38.

254. Bachelard, *Philosophy of No.*, p. 43.

255. Ibid., p. 41.

256. Ibid., p. 45.

257. Guéry, *L'épistémologie*, p. 131.

258. Ibid.

259. Ibid.

260. Ibid.

261. Ibid., p. 132.

262. Henri Bergson, "Einführung in die Metaphysik" in *Materie und Gedächtnis und andere Schriften* (Frankfurt am Main, 1964), p. 34; cf. also p. 35 [in English, *An Introduction to Metaphysics*, trans. T. E. Hulme (New York and London, 1912).]

263. Guéry, *L'épistémologie*, p. 132.

264. Ibid.

265. Ibid.

266. In his essay "Structuralist Activity" Roland Barthes writes that the "essence of every creation" is "technology." In *Critical Essays*, trans. Richard Howard (Evanston, 1972), p. 216.

267. Guéry, *L'épistémologie*, p. 132.

268. Cf. Fichant and Pécheux, *Sur l'histoire des sciences*, pp. 8–9. The positions cited here and in the following come from the definitions introduced by Pécheux and Balibar.

269. Cf. ibid., p. 9: "The discontinuist position takes exception to the notion of "knowledge" as a continuous development from 'common understanding' to 'scientific understanding,' from the dawn of science to modern science."

270. Ibid., p. 9. Here again one observes the overwhelmingly spatial metaphors of structuralism.

271. On Althusser's theory of ideology, one that falls behind Marx, see *For Marx*, p. 227, as well as my essay "Der strukturalistische Angriff auf die Geschichte," pp. 199–202.

272. Cf. Fichant and Pécheux, *Sur l'histoire des sciences*, p. 10.

273. Ibid. (emphasis in original).

274. Marx, *Capital*, 1:423 (emphasis in original).

275. Hegel, *Science of Logic*, p. 366.

276. Ibid., p. 370.

277. Ibid., p. 368.

278. Ibid., p. 374.

279. Ibid., p. 370.

280. Ibid., p. 372.

281. Ibid., p. 199.

282. On the intense contemporary discussion of continuous and discontinuous thinking, including contributions from researchers outside structuralism, see the instructive collection, *Das Problem der Kontinuität. Fünf Vorträge von Eike Haberland, Friedrich Kaulbach, Georg May, Gunther Mühle und Hans Schaefer*, ed. Peter Schneider and Otto Saame (Mainz, 1970). See also B. M. Kedrow, *Über Umfang und Inhalt eines sich verändernden Begriffs* (Berlin, 1956). Kedrow's work is oriented to Lenin's thesis that the history of the ideas of the separate disciplines condenses dialectical logic in concentrated form. He investigates the transition from quantitative to qualitative changes in the history of Mendelian concept of the elements.

283. Auguste Comte, *Cours de philosophie positive* (Paris, 1936). [For an English translation see *The Positive Philosophy of Auguste Comte*, freely trans. and condensed by Harriet Martineau (London, 1853).]

284. Ibid., p. 71.

285. Ibid., p. 72.

286. Ibid.

287. Ibid.

288. Oskar Negt in his doctoral dissertation, "Strukturbeziehungen zwischen den Gesellschaftslehren Comtes und Hegels" (Frankfurt am Main, 1964), investigated the complex relationship between early positivism and dialectical thinking in a very instructive manner. Cf. on this question Iring Fetscher's introduction to his German translation of Comte's *Discours sur l'Esprit Positif* (Paris, 1844), *Rede über den Geist des Positivismus* (Hamburg, 1956), p. xvi.

289. Hegel, *Lectures on the Philosophy of History*, 3:176.

290. Ibid.

291. Marx, *Capital*, 1:102.

292. Cf. on this the important work by W. S. Wygodski, *Die Geschichte einer grossen Entdeckung* (Berlin, 1967), especially p. 117.

293. Karl Marx, *The Poverty of Philosophy* (New York, 1976), p. 167.

294. Marx, *Grundrisse*, introduction, pp. 107–108 (emphasis in original).

295. Marx, *Contribution to the Critique*, p. 57.

296. Ibid., p. 19.

297. On this point cf. what Engels wrote in the preface to the third edition of *Capital* on Marx's rarely understood manner of quoting: "Hence these quotations are only a running commentary to the text, a commentary borrowed from the history of economic science. They establish the dates and originators of certain of the more important advances in economic theory. And that was a very necessary thing in a science whose historians have so far distinguished themselves only by the tendentious ignorance characteristic of place-hunters." Engels, preface to 3rd ed., *Capital*, 1:108.

298. Comte, *Rede über den Geist des Positivismus*, p. 5.

299. Ibid., pp. 41–51.

300. Ibid., pp. 203, 209.

301. Ibid., p. 211.

302. Ibid.

303. Lenin emphatically pointed this out in his conspectus of Hegel's lectures on the philosophy of history. See Lenin, *Philosophical Notebooks, Collected Works* (Moscow, 1961), vol. 38, pp. 245–315.

304. G. W. F. Hegel, *The Philosophy of History*, trans. J. Sibree and introd. C. J. Friedrich (New York, 1956), p. 10.

305. Ibid., p. 8.

306. Ibid., p. 10.

307. G. W. F. Hegel, *Philosophie der Weltgeschichte* (Leipzig, 1944), p. 10.

308. Ibid., p. 132.

309. Ibid., p. 133.

310. Ibid., p. 132.

311. Ibid., p. 133.

312. Ibid., p. 25.

313. Ibid.

314. Ibid., p. 55.

315. Ibid.

316. Ibid., p. 27; cf. also p. 29.

317. Ibid., p. 9.

318. Ibid., p. 25.

319. Ibid., p. 53 (emphasis in original).

320. Hegel writes in ibid., p. 50, "Spirit is essentially the result of its activity: its activity is the transcendance of immediacy, the negation of immediacy and return into itself."

321. Lukács, *History and Class Consciousness*, p. 157. Already in *The Poverty of Philosophy* Marx criticized this hostility to history (*Geschichtsfeindlichkeit*) in bourgeois social science: "When the economists say that present-day relations—the relations of bourgeois production—are natural, they imply that these are the relations in which wealth is created and productive forces developed in conformity with the laws of nature. These relations therefore are themselves natural laws independent of the influence of time. They are eternal laws which must always govern society. Thus there has been history, but there is no longer any. There has been history, since there were the institutions of feudalism, and in these institutions of feudalism we find quite different relations of production from those of bourgeois society, which the economists try to pass off as natural and as such, eternal." Marx, *The Poverty of Philosophy*, p. 174. It is noteworthy that in *Capital*, Marx comes back to precisely these considerations, now, however, within an accomplished analysis of the commodity. Now Marx derives the antihistorical character of bourgeois economic (as well as everyday) thinking from a social formation in which "the process of production has mastery over individuals, and man"—as a unified, self-conscious species-subject—"has not yet mastered the process of production." Marx, *Capital*, p. 175. Seen in this light, unhistorical thinking is the inability to analyze the existing condition from the perspective of its future mastery through solidary, acting individuals.

322. Lukács, *History and Class Consciousness*, p. 157 (emphasis in original).

323. Ibid., p. 159.

324. Ibid.

325. Marx, *Grundrisse*, introduction, pp. 107–108.

326. Lukács, *History and Class Consciousness*, p. 159. Here we should recall Marx's statement in *Capital*, 1:493: when referring to Vico he asserted that "human history differs from natural history in that we have made the former, but not the latter."

327. Maurice Godelier, *System, Struktur und Widerspruch im "Kapital,"* German trans. Joseph Grahl (Berlin, 1970), p. 14.

328. Ibid., p. 15.

329. Ibid. Cf. also p. 18 where Godelier once again develops these ideas and thus unfolds the main viewpoint of his structuralist exegesis of Marx: "The object of economic theory is to exhibit functions and their order in this or that structure and to determine the categories which follow from this structure . . . and to connect them to one another in a kind of logical, ideal genesis. But this genesis is not the actual history of formation. It cannot be a substitute for it. Further, economic theory, without coinciding with the history of the economy, supplies the guiding threads for the analysis of the latter, and is in its own development wholly based on the results of the latter. From this perspective, one can perhaps understand Marx's rigorous rejection of every kind of historicism or every effort to claim priority of historical over structural research . . . . a rejection that preceded the crises in sociological and linguistic circles (which led Saussure and Lowie's to give up evolutionary method) by more than fifty years."

330. Lukács, *History and Class Consciousness*, p. 159.

331. Marx, *The Poverty of Philosophy*, p. 162.

332. Ibid.

333. Ibid., p. 169.

334. Ibid.

335. Ibid., p. 170.

336. Characteristic of this widespread position (one to which I was at first inclined) is the study, generally worth reading, by Günter Kröber, "Die Kategorie 'Struktur' und der kategorische Strukturalismus," in *Deutsche Zeitschrift für Philosophie* vol. 16, no. 11 (Berlin, 1968): 1310–1324. Kröber describes "categorical structuralism" as a "philosophical position which dissolves the dialectical unity of structure and process in objective reality in favor of structure: not processes, but rather structures alone, not becoming, but rather that which has become . . . are worth investigating. For categorical structuralism, structure and elements do not exist as a dialectical unity in a system. Rather, the structure is the primary and determining phenomenon, which is supposed to have a self-sufficient existence that precedes and is independent of the elements and of the system," (ibid., p.

1317). Elsewhere Kröber writes on Marx's method in *Capital*, "Thus Marx never stops . . . at the point of dissolving the capitalist social formation into its structures. Although he does analyze the structure of capitalist society, at the same time he presents it as the result of a historical process which is itself determined in turn to be historically transcended. In *Capital*, of course, he undertakes a structural analysis of the capitalist mode of production but, in so doing, does not neglect either the critical analysis or the genesis of this mode of production, or the wealth of concrete, economic data" (ibid., p. 1319). In an abstract, purely descriptive sense, Kröber's objections against structuralism are as acceptable as are his positive statements concerning the method of *Capital*. However, on this very provisional level of discussion, one will never succeed in placing the legitimate kernel of the historical problematic raised by structuralism into the field of vision. Even more importantly, one is just as little able to derive the structuralist "hostility to history" out of a real "freezing" of historical movement.

Lucien Goldmann, who with the well-known psychologist Jean Piaget, distinguished "static" from "genetic structuralism" argued on lines similar to Kröber. See Lucien Goldmann, *Le Structuralisme* (Paris, 1968). Goldmann characterized dialectical materialism as "general, genetic . . . structuralism," for which "every human given is a meaningful structure which can be understood through an analysis of the essential connections between *its* individual elements . . . and simultaneously represents a constitutive element . . . of more comprehensive structures which encompass it. Viewed from this perspective, every human-given reality possesses a dynamic character and is first comprehended only when we have brought to light its past development and its inner constitutive tendencies directed toward the future. This points to the conclusion that the investigation of the given must always work out two mutually complementary sides of a process: The *destructuration* of a former structure and the *structuration* of a new structure in the process of emergence." Lucien Goldmann, *Dialektische Untersuchungen*, German trans. Ingrid Peters and Gisela Schöning (Neuwied/Berlin, 1966), p. 284 (emphasis in original). Disregarding for a moment the fact that it may be difficult to detect the concrete-critical content of Marxist theory behind this arid framework, Goldmann is trying to combine two complementary methods. Today outside of Marxism as well, there are efforts on all sides to accomplish this. Thus Werner Conze understands social history in the French image as "structural history of the technical-industrial era," quoted by Dietrich Hilger, "Zum Begriff und Gegenstand der Sozialgeschichte," in *Buch und Bibliothek*, vol. 23, no. 1 (Reutlingen, 1971): 21. Niklas Luhmann's structural-functional theory of social systems works with the concept of a "system-history" (*Systemgeschichte*) whose legitimacy results from [the primacy] of the "sociological enlightenment over the enlightenment of reason." *Soziologische Aufklärung* (Opladen, 1971), p. 83; on the whole issue, cf. pp. 82–85.

Index